# Ministering Freedom
## from Occult Bondages

# Ministering Freedom
## from Occult Bondages

Doris M. Wagner,
General Editor

WAGNER
PUBLICATIONS

*Ministering Freedom From Occult Bondages*
Copyright © 2004
by Doris M. Wagner
ISBN 1-58502-039-7

Published by
Wagner Publications
11005 Voyager Parkway
Colorado Springs, CO 80921
www.wagnerpublications.org


Cover design by
Imagestudios
100 East St. Suite 105
Colorado Springs, CO 80903
719-578-0351   www.imagestudios.net


Edit and Interior design by
Rebecca Sytsema

1   2   3   4   5   6   7   8   9     09   08   07   06   05   04

# Contents

# Meet the Contributors

While most Christians believe that demons exist somewhere in the world, a relatively small number of Christians realize that demons can affect their daily lives; and even fewer know how to effectively deal with one. But that is changing! Over the past few decades there has been a great resurgence in both the understanding and practice of deliverance. Because there is a need to understand this type of ministry, I decided to offer a useful series of books to help both the local church and the average Christian be equipped to effectively minister freedom from demonic oppression. Each book in the series deals with a specific topic. In an effort to help bring freedom to those entangled in the occult, and to equip those who minister to such people, I have invited some of my very special friends to contribute chapters to this book. Each one (with the exception of Frank Hammond) has come out of a background of the occult with its consequences and I have asked them to share their testimonies.

## Doris M. Wagner

I start off the book with a general overview of the occult, setting the stage for the rest of this book. I briefly review how Satan operates through the occult, including some explanation on a few forms, such as Eastern Religion.

## Frank D. Hammond

Frank Hammond, author of the classic book *Pigs in the Parlor*, was one of the forerunners of the deliverance movement. Many of us deliverance ministers have learned much of what we know from Frank and are greatly indebted to him for blazing the modern deliverance trail. We refer to Brother Frank as the "Dean of Deliverance."

## Chuck D. Pierce

In this book, Chuck D. Pierce shares how he came out of a family of spiritism and superstition. We consider Chuck to be one of America's foremost and accurate prophets. Chuck now heads up the United States Strategic Prayer Network and is leading our nation in the mobilization of strategic prophetic intercessors and various prayer initiatives.

## Araceli Alvarez

Araceli Alvarez is a close personal friend who came out of Cuban Santería, a powerful form of the occult. She rose to the level of high priestess and as such earned excellent money as she served others through that craft. She knows how to go after the demons with great accuracy, because she understands rituals, the use of curses, potions and even blood sacrifices. She now has her own deliverance ministry in Pasadena, California.

### Jeff Harshbarger

Jeff Harshbarger's testimony of his escape from Satanism is a miraculous story. His great desire is to expose the tactics of the devil, to warn people of the Church of Satan's dangers, and to deliver them from the dreadful snare of Satan worship. He currently helps people find freedom and gets them back on the right track after coming out of Satanism.

### Chris Hayward

Chris Hayward leads the large Cleansing Stream Ministries, a ministry of deliverance in over 3,500 (and growing) churches around the world. In this book Chris tells how he became involved in Eastern Religions and New Age. Chris explains what lures people into New Age with all of its deception and pitfalls, how he was freed, and pathways to freedom for those involved in New Age thinking.

### Ana Mendez Ferrell

Ana Mendez Ferrell was a high priestess of Voodoo, one of the most satanic religions on planet earth. She is now one of God's choice servants and has become a huge threat to the devil because she knows his tactics so very well. She is very familiar with the strengths and limitations of Satan and his demons, and, like a five-star general, she wages a fierce spiritual battle and wins. She spends a lot of her time training others for spiritual warfare.

**Chapter One**

# Shedding Light in the Darkness of the Occult

## Doris M. Wagner

Doris Wagner along with her husband, C. Peter Wagner, founded Global Harvest Ministries in 1992, with a vision of bringing together prayer networks for the purpose of focusing their collective prayer power on world evangelism. Doris serves in Global Harvest Ministries as the CEO. A deliverance minister for 20 years, she has helped set countless people free from various addictions and bondages. Because of her desire to see mobilization for deliverance within the church, she now specializes in deliverance training, speaking at regional and national conferences, and has taught practical seminars in many nations of the world. Her books and teaching resources are available by calling 888-563-5150, or at www.arsenalbooks.com.

Witchcraft, Satanism, Eastern Religions, and the occult in many forms are rapidly on the rise the world over. It seems as though Satan is working fast and furiously in these days, probably because he knows his time is short.

In his pride, Satan rose up against God because he wanted worship for himself. And to this day, his agenda remains the same. There is a kingdom of God and there is a kingdom of Satan; a kingdom of light and a kingdom of darkness.

Satan and his dark angels continually labor to rob Jehovah God of worship and devotion and usurp it for themselves. They must do so by deceiving people and leading them into the kingdom of darkness. They try to get a person to ask them for favors and, in so doing, bondages are created. The ensnared person becomes dependent upon these dark angels and returns to them over and over for power, guidance, and the satisfaction of personal desires. Thus the dark forces are getting the attention (tantamount to worship and service) they so strongly desire.

I have prayed for many people who have been caught in the trap of witchcraft and the occult, but have found their way out of the darkness into the glorious light of the truth and freedom from bondages. But it takes the light of the gospel shining into the darkness of the hidden occult to unmask the deception.

## Encounters with Cockroaches

I well remember, as a young missionary in the jungles of eastern Bolivia, being introduced to huge cockroaches for the first time. I was raised in a very temperate climate in the Mohawk Valley of New York State in a household run by a very clean German mom. I had never even seen a cockroach in my life because I never traveled far away from our dairy farm.

How well I recall my early encounters with cockroaches! Because there was no running water in our entire little Bolivian village, naturally there was no indoor plumbing, so we used outhouses as toilets. These were usually located quite a distance from living quarters for obvious reasons. Without the blessing of electricity either, at night we would need to carry a flashlight or a Coleman gasoline lantern to the outhouse to illuminate the path. There could be many nocturnal and potentially deadly "creepy crawlies" along the way.

The first few times I took the evening stroll, I used a flashlight and didn't see much on my journey. But when I took a Coleman lamp – what a different story! Things would scamper away and shun the light. But my biggest shock came when some of the strong light illuminated the entire interior of the outhouse, including what was down in the hole. Everything was teeming with cockroaches of various sizes – hundreds and hundreds of them. I then realized what they ate, and didn't cherish the thought very much.

But then I walked back the several hundred feet to our house. On the way, I passed our kitchen area, which was just a lean-to structure built to allow the heat of the kitchen to escape while we were cooking. Because of the lack of cupboard space, many items were hung on the walls on nails. You can imagine my shock and dismay when the bright light hit those walls and hundreds and hundreds of cockroaches scampered to take cover behind breadboards, wooden bowls, frying pans, and other hanging utensils I had used that day. My thoughts flashed back to the outhouse. Horrors!

Those little guys each had six dirty little feet and one dirty little mouth and they were lapping up bits of grease and food from my kitchen floor. I kind of wondered where they all slept during the day, because unless one opened a drawer or a cupboard door, they were pretty much out of sight and hence out of mind.

It's the same way when shedding light on the occult and demonic activity in a person's life. When the bright light from the kingdom of God shines on the deep darkness of the occult, the evil creatures and their activities are exposed and they can no longer remain hidden. Let's make no mistake about it – where there is occult activity there are many demons because those who engage in the occult summon up, use, and are then stuck with demons. It just comes with the territory!

But just as with cockroaches, simply exposing the demonic activity is not enough. For example, in a jungle lean-to kitchen, it took definite action to beat them back and finally get rid of them. It took powerful bug spray, thoroughly cleaning the utensils and area of infestation, and vigilance in keeping it clean. It was necessary to keep bread and other food in tightly covered tins, jars, boxes, or other appropriately sealed containers. Even dirt floors needed to be swept and kept free from food particles.

The desire for freedom from the occult on the part of the infested person, as well as thorough deliverance and inner healing, are needed to rid that person of demons. In my experience, I have found that demons simply do not leave on their own when exposed – they go into hiding for the time being, but come out in all their ugliness "at a more opportune time." They need to be commanded to leave in the name of Jesus. Their source of subsistence, and by that I mean the reason why they are there, needs to be removed and the environment where they had taken up residence must be thoroughly cleansed.

## What is the Occult?

That brings us to the meaning of the word occult. By occult I mean those who believe in, and practice in secret, the use of demonic powers to help bring to pass their often-evil wishes. Witches and warlocks, for example, fall into this category. Through the use of these demonic beings, they attempt to manipulate circumstances in order to bring about harm, such as sickness, calamity, and even death, to specific persons. They have the ability to use any combination of tools such as potions, chanting, rituals, magic, sorcery, effigies, the "evil eye," consecrated candles, incense, herbs, and geometrical shapes to cast spells and to curse. The occult practitioner's desire is often to gain power or control over others. What is a curse or a spell? Here is a quote from a tiny book entitled *Witches* by Kevin Osborn, from a witch's point of view:

"Spells, whether spoken or written, are not unlike prayers employed in most religious traditions. Both involve the invocation of spirits, deities, and other supernatural forces in order to achieve a desired end: love, power, a cure for illness, prosperity, fertility, or long life. Spells can divine the future, make a person invisible, permit astral projection (out-of-body experiences), or promote alchemy (e.g., turning lead into gold). They can also guard against various illnesses and disasters. Yet spells can equally be used to achieve more wicked ends. Witches became notorious for throwing powerful curses that brought ill fortune, loss of love, impotence, barrenness, sickness, or even death." (*Witches*, Kevin Osborn. Kansas City: Ariel Books 1996, pps. 36-38.)

That pretty much says it all!

It is not uncommon to see witchcraft turned into a very lucrative business. As others see that these practitioners have power, they are usually paid for their services. For a certain price, a witch will agree to perform a ritual, curse, hex, vex, incantation, or the like. As Osborn's definition above states, the most common reasons for a consultation usually include matters involving desires for money, health, love or sex, and power or control over others.

## Satan and his dark angels continually labor to rob worship and devotion to Jehovah God and usurp it for themselves.

The name given to occult practitioners will vary from place to place and culture to culture, depending upon the type of occult activity involved. Some of the more common terms that surface include, but are certainly not limited to: witches (females), warlocks (males), sorcerers (those who befriend demons and get them to act), spiritists, magicians, necromancers (who claim to speak with the dead in séances), spiritual healers also known as *curanderos* or witchdoctors, practitioners of Voodoo, Santería, Macumba, Umbanda, and workers of divination (these are many, just a few of which are: crystal ball users, readers of tea leaves, palm readers, tarot card readers, psychics, fortune tellers, and teachers of Feng Shui).

## The Invasion of Eastern Religions

Invading the American culture at the present time is the ever-increasing influence of Eastern Religions. Make no mistake about it, this has produced a proliferation of demonic activity. Sneaking into our homes, schools, businesses, hospitals, and universities are teachings on yoga, ungodly meditation, Wicca, mind control, hypnosis, and martial arts. Most Americans do not understand that involvement in such activities can open a door to demonic operation, and even oppression, in their lives and homes.

Because so many are being very deceived by them, let me speak briefly about a few practices of Eastern Religions.

Within the martial arts there is a variety of fighting sports that have their roots in ancient Eastern Religion, including Buddhism and Taoism. The religious significance of these arts lies in the harmonizing of life forces (Yin and Yang) and the ability to harness "Ch'i" (universal energy). Masters in the martial arts accomplish tremendous physical feats. I am convinced that these feats are accomplished with demonic help. I have frequently had to cast out spirits of violence and false religion from those who have practiced martial arts.

Transcendental Meditation (T.M.) comes from Hinduism and simply uses modern scientific terminology. While meditating, one chants a "mantra" which has personally been assigned to that person at the initiation ceremony. This ceremony is a ritual, offering worship to Hindu gods, and invokes their favor and presence. T.M.

offers an advanced program, which allegedly teaches students the ability to fly, levitate, and become invisible.

I once was praying deliverance over a young man who was struggling severely with lust.  In college he had taken a course in T.M., "just for the fun of it," and learned to meditate.  I asked him what his mantra was and he wrote it down on a piece of paper.  I knew a lady from India and took the piece of paper to her.  When she read the name she gasped and said it was the name of one of the most filthy, sexual goddesses in Hinduism.  Was there any wonder this fellow struggled with lust after invoking the name of a lustful, demonic spirit thousands of times over?  I was able to easily cast it out when we knew why it was there – it had simply been invited!  He was never told the meaning of the mantra or that it was worship of that goddess.

One of the most popular practices of Eastern Religion is yoga. The word and concept of yoga comes out of Hinduism and means "the path followed so as to realize the god within."  It involves the use of special postures and positions, along with meditation, to produce an altered state of consciousness, and ultimately, to achieve union with a god.  All forms of yoga involve the occult, even those presented as physical and breathing exercises.  The advanced levels are concerned with a mastery of cosmic forces and the practice of spiritistic and magical rituals.  To empty one's mind is a loud invitation to a demon to slip in and set up house-keeping.

I am told that there is a particularly strong and evil demonic spirit that can be invited into a person during yoga and medita-tion.  It lodges in the spine, starting at the tailbone and moving all the way up and over the skull, terminating between the eyes, in the spot called the "third eye."  It is called  "Kundalini" and acts very much like a snake, causing its host to writhe and slither along the floor. That's a stiff price to pay for so-called "exercise."

## Avoiding the Traps

Just as Satan and his dark angels lust for power and worship, so also many people lust for power and sense a need to worship something that will help them get what they want. Mostly, they want things to go their way. When Christians want circumstances to change, they ask an all-powerful God whom they worship, to change them in accordance with His will. All too often, when unbelievers want circumstances to change, they will seek counsel and help from the occult and will worship gods, goddesses, nature, and idols. In many instances, they will become harmed and possibly enslaved. Unless they turn from these practices, come to Christ, and get delivered, Satan has successfully exchanged some of his power for their worship.

The rate at which young people are entering the occult is alarming. They usually lack the knowledge of the Word of God, or have no respect for it. Deuteronomy 18:9-14 contains God's very clear instructions to His people concerning the occult:

"When you come into the land which the Lord your God is giving you, you shall not learn to follow the abominations of those nations. There shall not be found among you anyone who makes his son or his daughter pass through the fire, or one who practices witchcraft, or a soothsayer, or one who interprets omens, or a sorcerer, or one who conjures spells, or a medium, or a spiritist, or one who calls up the dead. For all who do these things are an abomination to the Lord, and because of these abominations, the Lord your God drives them out from before you. You shall be blameless before the Lord your God. For these nations which you will dispossess listened to soothsayers and diviners; but as for you, the Lord your God has not appointed such for you" (NKJV).

These instructions were given for the good of God's people, as guidelines to keep them from sin and the resulting personal problems. They are very clear. To obey is to keep clear of Satan's traps. Remember that his mission on earth is to steal, kill, and destroy. There is absolutely no such thing as good witchcraft or "white magic." That is a lie from the pit of hell. Dabbling is very dangerous and often opens a door for demons, who come to stay.

But, when God sets a person free from witchcraft and Satanism, he or she is "free indeed!" You are going to enjoy reading these stories and you will be filled with faith anew as you once again see what a great and wonderful, mighty and powerful God we serve. He is more than able to deliver us!

Together let us raise our hearts and voices and say: "Jehovah, God Almighty, You are the Lord our God, and we will have no other gods before you. We praise, adore, love, and worship you, now and for all of our days!" Amen.

# Chapter Two

# Breaking Witchcraft Curses

## Frank D. Hammond

Frank Hammond has been a pastor and teacher in the body of Christ for fifty-five years. Frank is a graduate of Baylor University and Southwestern Baptist Theological Seminary. He and his wife, Ida Mae (who has gone to be with the Lord), traveled and ministered throughout the United States and internationally with a major emphasis on spiritual warfare and family relationships. The Hammonds are authors of *Pigs in the Parlor, A Practical Guide to Deliverance*, and seventeen other books on various facets of deliverance. Frank's ministry, The Children's Bread, can be contacted at P.O. Box 789, Plainview, TX 79073-0789.

There are two spiritual power sources: God and Satan. Servants of the Most High God use their delegated spiritual authority to bless others and to defeat the devil. Emissaries of Satan employ Satan's power to curse, control, and harm. This supernatural evil power over people and their affairs is known as witchcraft or sorcery. God's Word absolutely condemns and forbids all witchcraft practices and involvement:

"Let no one be found among you who sacrifices his son or daughter in the fire, who practices divination or sorcery, interprets omens, engages in witchcraft, or casts spells, or who is a medium or spiritist or who consults the dead. Anyone who does these things is detestable to the LORD, and because of these detestable practices the LORD your God will drive out those nations before you" (Deut. 18:10-12, NIV).

Witches and wizards were condemned to death under the Law of Moses (see Lev. 20:27). God's Word is emphatic in condemning all that today is called "the black arts." Control of others is witchcraft's appeal. The witch and wizard, and those who seek after them, attempt to control others, endeavoring to gain some advantage over others. The power is real, but it is the devil's power, and its end is ruin. The history of Israel records times when God's people ignored God and turned to the powers of darkness for help. They thought that the sorcerers would solve their crises. God rebuked and judged Israel for relying upon witchcraft:

"When men tell you to consult mediums and spiritists, who whisper and mutter, should not a people inquire of their God? Why consult the dead on behalf of the living? To the law and to the testimony! If they do not speak according to this word, they have no light of dawn. Distressed and hungry, they will roam through the land; when they are famished, they will become enraged and, looking upward, will curse their king and their God" (Isa. 8:19-21, NIV).

The influence of witchcraft has increased in our own nation and society in recent years. "The whole world lieth in wickedness" (1 Jn. 5:19, KJV), for "the great dragon...that old serpent, called the Devil, and Satan...deceiveth the whole world" (Rev. 12:9, KJV). God said that the devil would deceive the whole world, and we are seeing it fulfilled.

The devil's deceptions are also infiltrating the body of Christ. Witchcraft is spreading into many local fellowships through New Age influences. Many Christians are turning to powers other than God in search of healing, guidance, and power.

We were invited to minister in church in a small Texas city. Before the service began, we noticed eight or ten people lined up in front of a man who seemed to be laying hands on them for healing. To our dismay, we learned that the man was dealing in Myotherapy, a form of acupressure. He was pressing the palms of people's hands to heal them. This was routinely taking place in the aisle of a charismatic fellowship. The leadership of the church had questioned the practice and was relieved when we brought it into the light of God's Word.

Our burden for the church today is expressed by Paul's concern over the church at Corinth: "But I am afraid that just as Eve was deceived by the serpent's cunning, your minds may somehow be led astray from your sincere and pure devotion to Christ" (2 Cor. 11:3, NIV).

> # Brave soldiers of the Cross are not awed by the devil. They know their weapons and their authority.

Witches employ incantations, potions, herbal concoctions, and other magical arts to bring about curses.  There are many plausible accounts of people who have suffered and even died due to witchcraft curses sent against them.

A couple, who were classmates of ours in seminary, went to Africa as missionaries.  Their first letter to us from Africa related their awe over the power of witchdoctors to afflict people with curses.  They had seen people die from such curses.  Their seminary training had not prepared them to confront these evil spiritual powers.

Most Christians today would consider it unbelievable that witchcraft would have such power.  Ezekiel prophesied to women who were doing some kind of witchcraft or voodoo:

"Woe to the women who sew magic charms on all their wrists and make veils of various lengths for their heads in order to ensnare people.  Will you ensnare the lives of my people but preserve your own?  You have profaned me among my people for a few handfuls of barley and scraps of bread. By lying to my people, who listen to lies, you have killed those who should not have died and have spared those who should not live" (Ezek. 13:18-19, NIV).

## Some Case Studies

Following are some case studies of deliverance needed as a result of occult activity:

### Maria

Maria needed deliverance. A couple in our church brought her to us. She was a very nervous, fearful, and distraught individual who was tormented by severe headaches. Maria was from Venezuela, South America. She had met and married a man from the United States. He was employed by an American oil company doing work in Venezuela.

In a pre-deliverance counseling session, we learned that Maria was a young believer in Christ whose family in Venezuela was deeply involved in witchcraft. She, her sister, and her mother had held hands, standing in a circle, and made a pact that they would never be separated. When Maria accompanied her husband to the States, her mother and sister put curses on her for breaking her vow. Maria explained that her mother kept a live owl, bat, and tarantula spider as instruments for putting curses on people.

When we commanded the demons to leave Maria, a spirit of death manifested by cutting off her breath, and her face contorted grotesquely as the demons were cast out. Deliverance from witchcraft spirits is often accompanied by strong manifestations. We were thankful that Maria started coming to our fellowship meetings to receive teachings that would help her to maintain her deliverance. She was a changed person. The powers of witchcraft had been defeated.

## James

James, a young soldier, was another person delivered from witchcraft curses. We met him at a deliverance conference we were conducting in California. James was a native of Jamaica. His father, uncle, and he were deeply involved in voodoo. Then, James became a Christian, and, being uncomfortable with his family's heavy occult activities, moved to the United States to get away from that influence. We found James to be very tormented and oppressed. An evil spirit came upon him every night and attacked him sexually. We explained that this spirit is called "succubus," a female demon that comes at night to sleeping males and gives them the sensation of having sexual relations. (The male counterpart to *succubus* is *incubus*, an unclean spirit that comes at night to lie on sleeping women in order to have sexual intercourse with them.)

A feeling of uncleanness overwhelmed James. He had tried everything he knew to get release from this tormenting spirit, but to no avail. In his ignorance of the demonic supernatural realm, he had consulted a witch in New England where he was then stationed in the army.

The witch instructed him to go home and get an egg. He was to bring the egg in his hand, traveling quite a distance on a bus. The egg must not be broken. The witch performed a ritual over the egg. She then instructed James to place the egg on the floor, and crush it with his foot. If a serpent came out of the egg it would be a sign that he was set free from the succubus.

James did as he was instructed, and, when he crushed the egg, out came a serpent! However, he soon discovered that the succubus was stronger than ever. His going to the occult for help only compounded his problem. Satan does not "cast out Satan" (see Matt. 12:26).

We led James in a prayer of confession and renunciation of the sins of witchcraft. In the mighty name of Jesus, we cast out the spirit of succubus and many other evil spirits. "If the Son therefore shall make you free, ye shall be free indeed" (Jn. 8:36, KJV).

We took time to teach James how to use his own spiritual authority as a believer in Jesus Christ. He then knew that should any of the spirits try to return, he could drive them away in the name of Jesus.

## Rita and Alberto

We began to learn firsthand about witchcraft curses while pastoring in a city with a strong Mexican-American culture that is steeped in witchcraft. We were reaching people for Christ out of this culture, and most of them had major problems from witchcraft curses.

A ringing phone jarred us out of a deep sleep. A glance at the clock told us that it was 2:00 am. It was Rita, a young woman who had attended a few services at our church. She was very excited and very urgent. She wanted me to come to her house as quickly as possible.

When I arrived at Rita's home, I found her brother, Alberto, a husky farm laborer, lying on the couch. He was too weak to move. He seemed at the point of death. Rita had seen us cast demons out of people, and she had tried to cast demons out of her brother. She showed me marks on her legs where the demons had attacked her and bit her. She was hysterical.

I began to pray for Alberto. I commanded the spirits of witchcraft to release him. Within a few minutes he sat up and asked for food since he had not eaten since getting home from the farm.

I was reminded of the sons of Sceva who attempted to cast demons out of a demonized man "by Jesus whom Paul preacheth...And the man in whom the evil spirit was leaped on them and overcame them" (Acts 19:13,16). The sons of Sceva were not believers in Christ and, therefore, had no spiritual authority over demons.

This was Rita's problem. She was attempting to cast out demons in the name of the Jesus whom I had talked about. She did not yet have a personal relationship with Christ. Soon afterward, she gave her heart to the Lord and is now helping to minister deliverance to others.

## Lupe

Lupe was a new convert in our congregation. She lived with her mother and elderly grandmother. Lupe confided in us that her grandmother was a witch. She used stuffed animals and other paraphernalia to work her witchcraft.

When the grandmother died, Lupe asked me and another person to pray over their house. She and her mother were experiencing some strange things. Three or four hours after sweeping and dusting the house, it would be dirty again. When one of them would sit in grandmother's chair, something would prick their legs. They had examined the chair and found there was no natural cause for the pricking. Furthermore, there had been several apparitions of the grandmother since her death.

We two pastors went through the house room by room. Every item that had belonged to the grandmother, which might have been used for witchcraft, was destroyed. We anointed the walls with oil and commanded every spirit of witchcraft to get out. No closet or cabinet was overlooked. The cleansing of the house was effective. None of the problems recurred.

## Lessons From Balaam

There is a biblical account of attempted witchcraft from which we learn several valuable truths. It is the account in Numbers 22–24 of King Balak hiring Balaam to curse the Israelites. Balaam was a prominent sorcerer in the region who, because of his ability to effect curses, was considered worthy of substantial payment for his services.

The Israelites had come up out of Egypt, had defeated the Amorite kings, and were now camped on the borders of Moab. Balak, the Moabite king, was afraid. The only chance he could see of defeating the Israelites was for them to be cursed by Balaam. Witchcraft was a recognized way of gaining an advantage over others.

Balaam had a solid reputation of being able to curse people. His ability to impose curses on others was no mere superstition. King Balak testified, "I know that those you bless are blessed, and those you curse are cursed" (Num. 22:6). Yes, witchcraft curses are real! In spite of Balaam's lust for reward he could only speak blessings upon God's people. God sovereignly intervened and prevented Israel from being cursed. Moses testified:

"Nevertheless the LORD thy God would not hearken unto Balaam; but the LORD thy God turned the curse into a blessing unto thee, because the LORD thy God loved thee" (Deut. 23:5, KJV).

Why was Balaam unable to curse Israel? All unbelief and rebellion had been purged out of their midst. When the cloud moved, they moved. They were God's people, walking in obedience to Him. Therefore, they were blessed of God.

Balak became impatient and angry toward Balaam. Why had he not cursed Israel? Balaam announced: "How shall I curse, whom God hath not cursed? or how shall I defy, whom the LORD hath not defied?" (Num. 23:8, KJV).

What do we learn from Balaam's inability to curse Israel? When we are walking in total obedience before God, the curse cannot alight. All who qualify for God's blessings are immune from witchcraft curses.

We must not become paranoid, fearing that someone is putting curses on us. Our Protection from witchcraft is simply living in righteousness and holiness before God. Too, we must remain vigilant, for the devil is always roaming about as a roaring lion seeking whom he may devour.

In Numbers 25, we discover that the Israelites committed whoredom with the daughters of Moab. They also "bowed down to their gods" (Num. 25:2). The judgment of God fell upon Israel and 24,000 perished! Who was the devil's instrument? Balaam!

"Behold, these caused the children of Israel, *through the counsel of Balaam,* to commit trespass against the LORD in the matter of Peor, and there was a plague among the congregation of the LORD" (Num. 31:16, KJV, emphasis added).

## All the Protection We Need

Thank God, Christians today are learning their authority in Him. They are becoming wise in knowing how to protect themselves from witchcraft and how to cancel the powers of witchcraft.

How can Christians protect themselves from witchcraft curses? Our protection is in putting on the whole armor of God. It is all the protection required. As Christian soldiers, we must keep on the girdle of *truth*, the breastplate of *righteousness*, the helmet of *salvation*, and the shield of *faith*. Our feet must be shod with a readiness to proclaim the *gospel of peace* and wield the sword of the Spirit, which is the *Word of God* (see Eph. 6:13-17). The whole armor of God is our defense.

Brave soldiers of the Cross are not awed by the devil. They know their weapons and their authority. We must never tremble at the powers of witchcraft nor cringe at the threats they pose, but remain strong in the Lord and the power of His might. Jesus promised, "Behold, I give unto you power to tread on serpents and scorpions, and over all the power of the enemy: and nothing shall by any means hurt you" (Luke 10:19, KJV).

## Steps to Breaking Curses

For any who know, or think that they have been exposed to witchcraft and other occult curses, I urge the following prayers and confessions. I encourage you to act on each step by repeating the prayer/confessions aloud, and personalizing your prayers whenever appropriate:

**Step One: Affirm your relationship with the Lord Jesus Christ.** Overcome Satan with *"the word of your testimony"* (Rev. 12:11, KJV) which is *"the testimony of Jesus Christ"* (Rev. 12:17, KJV).

Prayer: Lord Jesus Christ, I believe with all my heart that You are the Son of God. You left Your throne of Glory in heaven and became a man. You lived in this world and were tempted in all things just as we are, yet without sin. Then, You went to the Cross and laid down Your life. Your precious blood was poured out for my redemption. You rose from the dead and ascended into heaven. You are coming again in all Your glory. Yes, Lord, I belong to You.

I am Your child and heir to all Your promises.  You are my Savior, my Lord, and my Deliverer.  Amen.

**Step Two:  Repent of all your sins (known and unknown).**
Ask God's forgiveness through Jesus Christ.

Prayer:  Heavenly Father, I come to You in an attitude of repentance.  I ask You to forgive me of each sin that I have committed – the ones I am aware of and those which I have not recognized.  I am sorry for them all.

**Step Three:  Renounce the sins of your forefathers.**
Prayer:  Heavenly Father, I confess the sins of my forefathers.  I now renounce, break, and loose myself and my family from all hereditary curses, and from all demonic bondage placed upon us as the result of sins, transgressions, and iniquities through my parents and all of my ancestors.

**Step Four:  Accept God's forgiveness, and forgive yourself.**
Prayer:  Heavenly Father, You have promised in Your Word that if I will confess my sins, You are faithful and just to forgive me and will cleanse me from all unrighteousness (1 Jn. 1:9).  I believe that You have forgiven me for Christ's sake.  Therefore, I accept Your forgiveness, and I forgive myself.

**Step Five:  Forgive all others who have ever trespassed against you.**
Prayer:  Lord, others have trespassed against me, but you have commanded me to forgive each person who has ever hurt me or wronged me in any way.  I now make a quality decision to forgive (name them, both living and dead).  Also, I bless each of these

whom I have forgiven and pray that they will have Your peace, joy, and love in their lives.

### Step Six:   Renounce all contact with cults, the occult, or false religions.

Prayer:  Father, I confess as sin and ask Your forgiveness for every involvement with cults, the occult, and false religions.  (Be as specific as possible.)  I confess having sought from Satan's kingdom the knowledge, guidance, power, and healing that should come only from You.  I hereby renounce Satan and all of his works.  I loose myself from him, and I take back all the ground that I ever yielded to him.  I choose the blessing and refuse the curse.  I choose life and not death.

### Step Seven:   Destroy all books, objects, and paraphernalia associated with any cult, occult, or false religious source.

Prayer:  Heavenly Father, You are a jealous God, visiting the iniquities of the fathers upon the children unto the third and fourth generation of them who hate you.  Therefore, I destroy all books and objects in my possession that are contrary to You and Your Kingdom.  If there is anything in my possession that is not pleasing to you and gives any advantage to the devil, reveal this to me, and I will destroy it.

### Step Eight:   Cast out every demon of curse.

Warfare Prayer:  Satan, you have no right to my life and no power over me.  I belong to God, and will serve Him and Him only.  By the authority of my Lord Jesus Christ, I break the power of every evil curse that has come upon me.  I command every demon of curse to leave me now:  ancestral curse spirits, personal transgression curse spirits, witchcraft curse spirits, and spoken word curse spirits. (Note:  Be as specific as possible in identifying spirits of curses.)

**Step Nine:  Claim the blessing.**  Now that the curses are broken, and the demons of curse have been cast out, it is time to confess your blessings in the Lord.  Know this:  The grace of God enables you to stand unashamed in the presence of God Himself. Since you have God's favor, you are assured of His blessings.

Prayer:  Heavenly Father, thank You for delivering me from every curse through the redemptive work of Your Son and my Savior, Jesus Christ.  You exalt me and set me on high.  You cause me to be fruitful and to prosper in everything.  By Your hand of blessing I am a success and not a failure.  I am the head and not the tail – above and not beneath.  You have established me in holiness.  I am Yours, and I purpose to serve You and to glorify Your name. (Note:  Those in headship should bless those under their care.  Let the pastor bless the people, the husband his wife, the parents their children.  I have found it especially effective and deeply appreciated, after deliverance from curses, to speak a pastoral or fatherly blessing upon the one[s] delivered.  It is a heart-moving experience for those who have never had a blessing spoken over them by persons in authority.)

God instructed Aaron and his sons to put His name upon the children of Israel and bless them.  Let us use these same priestly words to speak blessings upon others.

"The LORD bless thee, and keep thee:  The LORD make his face shine upon thee, and be gracious unto thee:  The LORD lift up his countenance upon thee, and give thee peace" (Num. 6:24-26, KJV).

Amen!

**Chapter Three**

# Blinding the Evil Eye

### Chuck D. Pierce

Chuck D. Pierce is Vice President of Global Harvest Ministries, President of Glory of Zion International Ministries, and Mobilizing Apostle for the U.S. Strategic Prayer Network. He has been used by God to intercede and mobilize prayer for local churches, cities, and nations. In addition, he coordinates prayer for many of the major spiritual events and gatherings around the world, and is a prophet to territories and cities. Chuck and his wife, Pam, live with their five children in Denton, Texas. He has authored several books including *Possessing Your Inheritance* and *Future War of the Church*. These and all of Chuck's materials are available through Glory of Zion at 888-965-1099 or by visiting www.glory-of-zion.org.

# A Blind Spot

I can still remember the eye doctor telling me, "You have a blind spot." A blind spot? What could that mean? He showed me the test results and there was a huge portion of my vision that was being blocked. *He called this a blind spot.* A blind spot is that small area which is insensitive to *light* in the retina of the eye.

Another definition of a blind spot is a person's lack of sensitivity to a particular thing. A blind spot can be a prejudice or ignorance over a subject – yet one may be unaware that this is within; and I knew the Lord was going to uncover whatever was hidden in me. I was diagnosed as either having a tumor on my optic nerve or a blood clot that was pressing on the nerve and blocking my vision. In any case, this seemed to be a serious enough for the doctors to want me quickly in the hospital for further testing.

Little did I know that God had planned a week of deliverance. The week turned into a year. The year turned into a process of ten years. The ten years resulted in a testimony of freedom. And the Lord let in a lot of light.

## The Lamp of the Body

Matthew 6:22-23 declares, "The lamp of the body is the eye. If therefore your eye is good, your whole body will be full of light. But if your eye is bad, your whole body will be full of darkness. If therefore the light that is in you is darkness, how great is that darkness!"

The eye is a major gate, where information is perceived and channeled into the human soul and spirit. In the Bible, one method of punishment in war was to blind or put out the eyes of the captive. If the eye is to be useful, it must see clearly. Biblically, the eye is of great importance for a person to prosper fully in God's plan. It also relates to the heart and mind, since the 'eye of the heart' determines our spiritual perception. If our spiritual eye is open, then we can receive enlightenment, and the Spirit of God can flow. If our eye is darkened, our whole body becomes dark and eventually we lose our way.

The Bible says we can be blinded by the deceptive ways of the enemy. "Occult" means to conceal or cause to disappear from view – to be secret, mysterious, supernatural. But God gives us access to revelation that will uncover that which has been kept secret.

The enemy likes to hide. He plans strategies to divert us from accomplishing God's will and entering into His blessings. Many of us have a hard time *seeing* the enemy's snares, strategically planted along our path. Thus, we *step into* his tangled web and spend much of our time struggling to free ourselves. We must ask the Lord to help us look past the visible to see the invisible, and any supernatural force that would ensnare us – keeping us from accomplishing the Lord's will.

## My Family had a Good Eye and a Bad Eye: How Generational Iniquity Blinds

Occult practices were not unusual in the generations of my family. I had seen occult power at work. There was an inherited weakness toward sins of the occult and witchcraft that were passed down through our bloodline. A weakness like this is known as *iniquity*. Iniquity forms a pattern in our life that causes us to deviate from God's perfect path. Its root definition is linked to "unequal" or "twisted." In other words, you do something that is not equal to God's righteous standard and you are unwilling to be reconciled to God's ways. This causes your path to be twisted.

I was soon to discover that this "blind spot" I was experiencing was linked to many inherited occult influences in my life. Have you ever noticed how such things as alcoholism, divorce, laziness, or greed, tend to run in families? These aren't just learned behaviors. They are manifestations of iniquity, or iniquitous patterns, passed down through the generations.[1] Occult iniquitous patterns work the same way, only they are more difficult to detect because they are hidden. When I entered the hospital, it was as if the Lord was pulling me aside so He could go deep down and show me some things that had been hidden for a long time.

My family had all the potential in the world to prosper. They were a good, hard-working, family. However, the enemy seemed to ravage and destroy all God had planned. I saw my dad being led astray and involved in gambling, and eventually witchcraft. As a child, the supernatural was easy for me to understand because I watched certain family members operate in supernatural dimensions. My grandfather could speak words and bring about changes in the elements around him. I had cousins who would visit with an unknown source and then watch the table rise up off the floor. I thought nothing about buying my first Ouija board when I was 10 years old. I was never told it was a game or harmless; I just knew I could ask it questions and it would speak back.

One side of my family was so steeped in superstition that all the rules became wearying to follow. Of course, I also had some family members who were totally devout, praying, godly saints. Talk about eyes unfocused and going in every direction!

## Familial and Familiar Spirits

My wife, Pam, would always tell me that there was something driving me to react at times. However, she could never put her finger on what it was. She would say, "It's linked to your family in some way. Every time we almost see what it is, it's like a bat that flies back into the cave. It never comes to the light enough to detect and pull out of you. Like the way certain members of your family operate!"

A family is defined as a group of people living in the same house, one or more people consisting of the same parents, or a group of people that have a common blood tie. Sin is an opening for demonic forces to work in subsequent generations of a family because of the iniquity produced. Spirits assigned to a family are called *familial spirits*. Some have been in families for generations.[2] They know the iniquitous patterns in a family bloodline. They know when it began. They know that, unless they are dealt with through the blood of Jesus, these iniquitous patterns will be passed on to someone else in the next generation.

*Familiar spirits* work the same way, only they do not have to be part of the family bloodline. "Familiar" is applied that which is known through constant association. They are linked with some sort of intimacy, such as sexual soul ties. The old saying, "birds of a feather flock together," does have some validity. The iniquitous pattern in one person is drawn to the iniquitous pattern in another. I call this a cluster of iniquity. If one member of the cluster dies or lets go of this iniquitous pattern, it reinforces its strength in the other members.

## Declaring that All Things Hidden Will be Revealed

I went to a cell group for prayer. One of the leaders, a very spiritual woman who had been involved in the occult, laid hands on me and declared that anything hidden within me would be exposed. Oh my, did this stir up a nest! It was as if my blood curdled, the bottom of the lake came to the top, and over time things began to expose themselves.

Soon after, I was trying to finish getting things done around our house before I went to the hospital. My wife has always kept a most beautiful yard, but she noticed a small brown spot in the grass. She asked if I could determine the cause of that spot. The brown spot was like my blind spot. The more I dug, the larger the hole got in our front yard. I became frustrated because I had dug a hole three feet wide while the spot looked to be only a couple of inches. I found a huge piece of concrete underneath our luscious green yard. It was not evident until the heat of August got to a certain level. When things heat up, reactions occur. Pam walked out and, of course, had a better way of digging so the yard would not be ruined. I felt this strange feeling come over me. (Doris Wagner always says this is one way to detect a demon – something *"comes over you."*) I felt like I was outside of my body. My natural self wanted the take the sledge hammer I was using and throw it as hard as I could at my wife. Thank God for wisdom and self-control – and a measure of fear, because I know my wife (she, too, can react!).

I stopped where I stood and said: "Lord, I've had this familiar feeling before. Remind me of when and how this happened." Immediately, the Lord reminded me of times when I would have what my grandmother would call a "spell." She would have me go lay down in a bedroom and chant certain words until the "spell" subsided. Instead of throwing the hammer, I went inside, laid down on my bed, and remembered every word of the chant. Instead of chanting, I renounced those words, and decreed that any power attached to them would no longer have the right to hold me captive. I prayed the blood of Jesus over me and my family, and asked God to fill me anew with His Holy Spirit. This was the beginning of true freedom.

## Which Eye is Watching Me: The Evil Eye?

"Evil eye" simply means seeing something from a perverse perspective. The Bible says it this way – we call good evil, and evil good. The evil eye is linked with most occult practices and secret societies. The evil eye "watches after its resources." Gambling is linked to an evil eye, as is all superstition. Many times this "evil eye" must be blinded so you can be free from the controlling, familial, or familiar spirit that is watching to keep you in bondage. The "eye of the heart" can be subverted by the "evil eye." The Bible warns against an evil eye. Prov. 23:6 says, "Eat thou not the bread of him that hath an evil eye, neither desire thou his dainty meats…" Covetousness is linked to an evil eye. Proverbs 28:22 says, "He that hasteth to be rich hath an evil eye, and considereth not that poverty shall come upon him." The evil eye is also linked with evil thoughts producing evil actions. In the Bible, the expression is synonymous with envy, jealousy, and some forms of covetousness. In Mark 7:20-23, an evil action begins with a single thought. Verse 22 says, "Thefts, covetousness, wickedness, deceit, lasciviousness, an evil eye, blasphemy, pride, foolishness…" Jesus said these things are within us and make us unclean.

## The Evil Eye and Mammon

Have you ever noticed your dollar bill? The evil eye is imbedded right there in the paper. We all know we can't burn and get rid of every dollar bill we have. So we have to ask God how to deal with this evil eye. In Deuteronomy 8:18, we find that as the Lord spoke to His covenant people and prepared them to go into the land He promised, He told them He would give them the power to get wealth. He knew they would be in spiritual war with Mammon. When you study Canaanite history, you find that their ruling god was Mammon. The assignment of Joshua and the tribes of Israel was to convert the wealth thereof to God's covenant Kingdom plan. Therefore, Mammon had to be defeated and the wealth held by its false worship transferred.

Because the evil eye is involved in our money system, we must guard ourselves against the *love of money* (1 Timothy 6:10). *Philarguria* refers to avarice, which is the insatiable greed for riches, covetousness; to inordinately or wrongly desire the possessions of others. If we are not careful, this is the fruit that money will produce in our hearts. And *deceitfulness of riches* (Mark 4:19) becomes an issue. This is primarily the perceived power that comes with money. It produces an attitude of the heart, seeking to manipulate through false pretenses and appearances.

Money often has curses attached to it. If you don't break the curse before you get the money, you will get the curse that comes with the money. There are a number of people in the Word who were cursed by wealth, or were driven by impure motives to gain it; for instance: Judas, Esau, Gehazi, Ananias and Sapphira, Lot, and Achan – they were trapped by their impure desires. Malachi 3 tells us that one way to break this curse is to tithe and give offerings; but most of all, to break the attitude. As we move forward against the enemy, we must renounce every issue of covetousness tied to Mammon and break its curses. Money is good when it is a servant to us. However, we can become slave to its dominion. Then it is truly an evil eye.

Envy is also linked with covetousness and the evil eye – envy as distinguished from jealousy. When we look at something or someone else with an unholy desire, especially their riches, we fall under the power of this demon's grip. The power of envy is stated in Prov. 27:4: "Who is able to stand before envy?" We must sanctify what God gives us and be satisfied with our portion.

## Superstition is a Sign – of Ignorance

Superstition is probably more closely linked with the evil eye than anything else. Superstition can actually mean "fearing demons." It is a belief, half-belief, or practice for which there appears to be no rational substance, but which supposedly brings you protection. Superstitions can fall into three categories: *religious, cultural,* and *personal.* A religious superstition (against which Christians are not immune) may be something like leaving an open Bible next to a bed to gain protection from demons. Cultural superstitions are folk traditions linked to irrational beliefs intended to ward off illness, bring good, foretell the future, and prevent accidents.  A personal superstition may include needing to use a lucky pen or, when gambling, betting on a particular color of horse.  Superstition develops a mind-binding fear within.

My family was steeped in superstition.  Several of them really affected my life as I was growing up – they kept me in fear.  Here are a few examples, followed by how the Lord broke me out of that mindset:

## Bed

- ◆ It is bad luck to put a hat on a bed.
- ◆ If you make a bedspread, or a quilt, be sure to finish it or marriage will never come to you.
- ◆ When making the bed, don't interrupt your work, or you will spend a restless night in it.

Psalm 4:8 says, "I will lay down and sleep in peace; for you alone, O Lord, make me dwell in safety."  Claiming this Scripture was helpful in freeing me from the superstitions regarding the bed and rest.

## Broom

- ◆ Do not lean a broom against a bed.  The evil spirits in the broom will cast a spell on the bed.
- ◆ If you sweep trash out the door after dark, it will bring a stranger to visit.
- ◆ If someone is sweeping the floor and sweeps over your feet, you will have calamity.
- ◆ If you take a broom from one house to another, you will allow the spirits of the previous house to come.

- To prevent an unwelcome guest from returning, you should sweep out the room immediately and bind him from ever returning.

The Lord showed me that He stood at my door and knocked, and that I should always be willing to let Him in. He took me to Song of Solomon and Revelation and gave me Scriptures. He showed me that a broom had no power in itself, and that if an evil spirit entered my house I had the authority to bind and cast it out.

The next two were more difficult for me to overcome:

## Bird

- A bird in the house is a sign of death.
- If a robin flies into a room through a window, death will shortly follow.

The Lord showed me two things: first, according to Matthew 6, He loved me more than any bird; then He showed me Psalm 84 and said: "The swallow has a nest for herself where she may have her young, a place near your altar…" He showed me how to build an altar to Him in my home through prayer and worship so I need not fear any intrusion. Now if a bird comes into my house, it can be at home with God and me, because my house is a sanctuary.

## Cat

- If a black cat walks toward you, it brings good fortune, but if it walks away, it takes the good luck with it.
- Keep cats away from babies because they "suck the breath" of the child.
- A cat on board a ship is considered to bring luck.

♦ If a black cat crossed in front of you, you must turn around for trouble would be on the path ahead.

There were many times idiotic word curses like this would turn my family from the path they were on. I was late one day going to work because there was a black cat in the path I normally took. I was living fully in the Lord, however, words which had been a part of my belief system, would not die easily. They had built a stronghold. In the end, I just broke the devil's power – the words. Then I "heard a word from behind me telling me not to turn to the right nor the left, but to go forward." I was freed.

The next two phrases led me into obsessive-compulsive tendencies and created a fear of death within me.

## Crack

♦ Don't step on a crack on a sidewalk or walkway.

I made it through the crack obsession when I was 12. I just simply stepped on one. At that time, things weren't going too well, so what was one more issue? I believe the breaking of this curse was the beginning of my realizing how ignorant superstition was.

## Sparrow

♦ Sparrows carry the souls of the dead, and it's unlucky to kill one.

The sparrow curse was linked to the practice of spiritism in my family. For this, God gave me Prov. 26:2: "Like a fluttering sparrow or a darting swallow, an undeserved curse does not come to rest." In other words, the sparrow did not carry the soul of a human, nor could its death bring a curse upon my life or family.

## Spiritism and the Evil Eye

The evil eye also works through spiritism. Spiritism is the belief that the living can and do communicate with spirits of the dead. It includes the various practices by which such communication is attempted. There are phenomena that are of a physical nature that relate to the spiritual realm:

- production of raps and other sounds;
- movement of objects (tables, chairs) without contact or with contact insufficient to explain the movement:
- "apports" i.e., apparition of objects with no visible agency to convey them;
- moulds, i.e., impressions made upon paraffin and similar substances;
- luminous appearances, i.e., vague glimmerings, light, or faces more or less defined;
- levitation, i.e., raising of objects from the ground by supposed supernormal means;
- materialization or appearance of a spirit in visible human form;
- spirit-photography, in which the feature or forms of deceased persons appear on the plate along with the likeness of a living photographed subject.

The psychical, or significative phenomena are those which express ideas or contain messages. To this class belong:

- table-rapping in answer to questions;
- automatic writing; slate-writing;
- trance-speaking;
- clairvoyance;

- ◆ descriptions of the spirit-world; and
- ◆ communications from the dead.[3]

Spiritism can even take on a religious character. It is not that during spiritistic rituals and practices, such as séances, the dead actually "communicate back;" evil spirits linked with familiar and familial spirits communicate to individuals to reinforce their fears and guide them into twisted paths. In other words, the demon forces

> # We must ask the Lord to help us look past the visible to see the invisible, and any supernatural force that would ensnare us – keeping us from accomplishing the Lord's will.

that were with the dead individuals during their life will know the answers to questions and will pose as the dead one with whom the spiritist is trying to communicate.

This is a very dangerous and deceitful practice because it can seem so real – after all, who but the real Aunt Nellie could have known that rocky road was her favorite flavor of ice cream? The problem is that those who are attempting to communicate with Aunt Nellie aren't reaching her at all, but they are contacting and inviting the presence and counsel of the demons who tormented Aunt Nellie during her life.

But be assured that the only true outcome of these attempts to communicate is a wide open door to demonization by familial or familiar spirits. This practice can lead into delusion and eventually death.  The torment caused by these spirits can bring great mental imbalance and vexation.  Spiritism invites the evil eye and opens the soul to satanic influence and control.

## Magic and Sorcery

When we are looking at an occult relationship with the evil eye, we also must review how magic and sorcery attempt to influence people and events.  Biblically we find them linked with many aspects of the supernatural:  sorcery, witchcraft, magic, enchantment using charms, charmer, Chaldeans, divination, secret arts, enchantment using spells, snake charming, Magi or wise men, sorcery using drugs and potions, spiritual imposters, mind-binding spells, curious arts, and religious bewitchment.  Magic itself may be associated with some forms of divination.  Divination is the attempt to use supernatural means to discover events or information.

Magic is universal, and may be "black" or "white."  Black magic attempts to produce evil results through such methods as curses, spells, destruction of models of one's enemy, and alliance with evil spirits.  It often takes the form of witchcraft.  White magic tries to undo curses and spells, and to use occult forces for the good of oneself and others.  (Of course, in reality there is no good magic.  All magic is of Satan and leads to death, hell, and the grave).

The magician tries to compel a god, demon, or spirit to work for him.  He follows a pattern of occult practices to bend psychic forces to his will and the will of the one using him.  Magic and sorcery are not mere superstitions; they have a reality behind them.  And they must be resisted and overcome through the power of God through the Holy Spirit in the name of Jesus Christ.

# Freemasonry

The evil eye is very attached to ritualistic practices and secret societies. One powerful secret society that uses the evil eye to control its members is Freemasonry. In the short space here, a long explanation is not possible. However, Selwyn Stevens has a small, clear book called *Unmasking Freemasonry: Removing the Hoodwink,* in which he explains the dangers of Freemasonry.

There is much secrecy involved in this religion. This often opens a person to fear and bondage. Interestingly, Wicca and Mormonism have similar rites to those of Freemasons. The initiations that bring you into Freemasonry are humiliating. If you are married you have to remove your wedding ring because you have got to be totally "married or in covenant with" the words that you speak and the false god behind it. There is a wall of secrecy between a Freemason and his wife. This is how the occult works.

In Freemasonry, there are 33 degrees of attainable power and authority. In the Third Degree, a penalty is sworn by the mason to have his body cut in two, his bowels removed, and be burned to ashes and scattered to the four winds if he violates the Masonic brotherhood. There are oaths taken in every degree. These oaths in freemasonry are filled with curses that are attached to the generations. This is why it's so hard for anyone to get out of this false religion.

Those who are initiated live in constant turmoil, making blind contracts with the enemy by speaking things that can be very destructive in their life and the lives of future generations. Yet if a member tries to leave, he faces censure. Freemasons will not associate with one who has left the fold. They believe the sacred oaths have been broken. The person is then criticized and cursed, sometimes hounded; forever treated as untrustworthy.

Nevertheless, as Selwyn Stevens says, "God's Word requires a Christian to renounce a bad or sinful oath such as this. Leviticus 5:4-5 shows us that if a person is required to swear something which was hidden prior to the oath-taking, God says we should plead guilty to Him, confess it as sin and totally renounce and repudiate it, preferably publicly. When you have done this God says you are no longer bound by it. God wants us to know that repentance releases us from such a vow or oath. This is one of the major keys for removing the consequences of the curses invoked by Masonic oaths."[4]

## Remove the Evil One's Veil

Through this chapter you have begun to understand that the enemy clouds our ability to discern. He hides himself. He plots and plans to divert us from accomplishing God's will and entering into His blessings. Many of us have a hard time *seeing* the enemy's snare or diversion. Therefore, we often *step in* the middle of this tangled web, and spend much of our time struggling to free ourselves. Let me suggest 15 ways we can remove the enemy's hidden snares in our lives:

1. The enemy has a voice to bring deception into your life. Ask God to show you any deception or lie he has fostered.

2. Satan is the father of lies and can only work with any resource that we give him. Cut ties with anything in your soulish nature that is holding you captive.

3. Ask the Lord to fill you with His love so that you can break any sin strategy in your life and destroy the devil's work.

4. Jesus resisted the voice of the enemy. Ask the Lord to fill you with the Spirit in the midst of your wilderness so you also can resist him.

5. Do not be ignorant. Let God reveal to you the supernatural qualities that the enemy possesses – Lucifer's hidden characteristics.

6. Be sure you are operating in humility and submission so you can resist effectively.

7. Satan wants you to believe that God is not directing you; that He is holding out on you – he manipulates. Ask God to break any manipulation that is aligned with your desires.

8. Be sure your desires are aligned correctly. Temptation is linked to selfish desires that are not within God's boundaries.

9. Ask the Lord to deliver you from temptation.

10. Change your mind or redevelop your thought process (repent). Renounce acts linked with your wrong thinking. Forgive yourself and others who have seduced and led you astray.

11. Ask God to give you a mind for increase. Ask Him to open your heart to any prophetic word that will bring you success and cause you to be able to rake in the spoils that the enemy is holding.

**12.** Declare deliverance from the hand of the wicked who have robbed you of your provision and health.

**13.** Declare that the generational curse of "God-robbing" will be released from your bloodline. This is one of the four major generational curses. Tear down mindsets of poverty that might tell you, "God is not able." This is a lie to withhold that which should be freely given.

**14.** Dismantle unbelief over provision. "Prove Me *now*," says the Lord!  Look up and see the windows of blessing that He wants to open up. Watch Him overcome your devourer.

**15.** Rejoice that you are free from the enemy's plans and purposes!

Let your eye be filled with light, and may the Holy Spirit direct every step of your path. "The path of the righteous is like the first gleam of the dawn shining ever brighter until the full break of day" (Prov. 4:18).

***Notes***
[1] Taken from Chuck D. Pierce and Rebecca Wagner Sytsema, *Possessing Your Inheritance* (Ventura, CA:  Renew Books), pp. 172-173.
[2] Ibid., p. 174.
[3] http://www.newadvent.org/cathen/14221a.htm.
[4] Selwyn Stevens, *Unmasking Freemasonry: Removing the Hoodwink* (Jubilee Resources, Wellington, New Zealand: 1999), p. 19.

# Chapter Four

# My Escape from Santería

### Araceli Alvarez

Araceli has an extensive background in witchcraft, the occult, and New Age. Since her
conversion and subsequent deliverance, she
has become one of the leading experts on deliverance
from witchcraft, heading up Fountain of Freedom Ministries, a Christian prayer ministry which ministers to
believers who desire to be free from spiritual strong-
holds, demonic influences, recurring sin issues, soul
ties, rejection, deep emotional wounds that have resulted in dysfunction and bitterness, and other spiritual
bondages that prevent them from enjoying a close walk
with our Lord Jesus and experiencing the joy available
to all believers. Araceli can be reached by e-mail at
fountainfredom@aol.com or by phone at (818) 729-
7980.

I was born in Cuba and raised in a family who called themselves Roman Catholics. But like the majority of such families, we just went to church on special occasions. At the age of twelve, I became a good practicing follower of Catholicism. I became very deeply involved in the church – teaching catechism, working with food banks, distributing toys, giving blankets to the elderly and food to the needy, and serving in the Catholic Youth Organization. My time was divided between teaching my students and working in my church.

In 1958, I married a Cuban Air Force pilot. In 1959, Fidel Castro overthrew the Cuban government. This was a crucial and frightening point in my life because my husband, who was as an active pilot, was imprisoned.

Castro's government was holding military trials for just about any reason, and a person could be sentenced to 30 years of hard labor, or to death the next morning, being executed by a firing squad. No investigation or witnesses were needed. If someone said that you were not a follower of the revolution, that was enough. Castro condemned the Cuban pilots before any trials were held.  He just appeared in public and said they had to be judged and condemned "just to be an example to the rest of the world."

My mother always had believed in spiritism.  She suggested that under the circumstances I should go to a *santero* and seek help of the "saints."  I agreed out of desperation, fear, confusion, and the knowledge that justice was not available due to the political situation at that time.  I went for a "*consulta*," a reading, which was done by a priest with small river shells.  From that moment on, everything became a whirlwind.  I was told that I needed to be initiated in order to save the life of my husband and myself.  Without thinking, I paid the required fees and prepared myself for the initiation ceremony.  And thus, I entered into the world of Santería.  To understand, we need a little history.

## What is Santería?

Santería is a religious tradition of African origin that developed in Cuba at the beginning of the nineteenth century, when hundreds of thousands of men and women of the Yoruba people, from what are now Nigeria and Benin, were brought as slaves to Cuba to work in the island's booming sugar industry.  They were forced to convert to the Roman Catholic Church.  In spite of the terrible conditions, they were able to keep their own religious rites; associating the stories of different Catholic saints to their own gods' stories.  They used the statues that represented specific Catholic saints to worship their spirits called *orishas*, which are represented with different kinds of stones and river shells.

The name Santería means "the way of the saints."  The word *Sao* or *santera* indicates an initiated devotee.  Despite the frequent presence of Catholic symbols in Santería rites and the attendance of *santeros* at Catholic sacraments, Santería is essentially an African way of worship drawn into a symbiotic relationship with Catholicism. This explains why all Latin American countries so easily fall into the trap of this cult. The basis of Santería is the development of a deep personal relationship with the *orishas*, a relationship that will bring the *santero* worldly success and "heavenly" wisdom.

Devotion to the *orishas* takes four principal forms: divination, sacrifice, spirit mediumship, and initiation. For the ordinary devotee, Santería serves as a means for resolving the problems of everyday life, including problems of health, money, and love. Divination claims to reveal the source of these problems, and it points the way to their resolution. The different methods of divination that are used range from reading river shells by a *santero* to the complicated deep divination done by a *babalawo*.

The most complex system of divination in Santería, *ifa*, can be "read" only by male priests called *babalawos*. In response to an adherent's problem, a *babalawo* will throw a small chain (*ekwele*)

> **All the prayers may be in a dialect that they do not understand. Nevertheless, they are promising all of their life, family, finances, and faithfulness to the demonic *orisha*.**

that has eight pieces of shell, bone, or other material affixed to it. Each piece is shaped so that, when thrown, it lands either concave or convex side up. This results in 256 possible combinations, each representing a basic situation in life. The combination that falls at any particular time is considered to be the purest expression of fate, and is thus the God-given destiny of the devotee. Most of the patterns refer to stories that tell of the problems faced by the *orishas* and heroes in the past, and relate the solutions that were found. These solutions become the archetypes used by the devotee to resolve the problem.

As problems seem to be solved, the devotee becomes more deeply dependent on the *orisha*. As the dependence becomes greater and greater, the devotee's involvement soon includes offering sacrifices, being initiated, and finally dominated by the *orisha*. It was in this type of environment that I rose to the position of a high priestess.

## The Journey Into – and Out of – Santería

Finally my husband and twenty-seven other pilots were tried. He was sentenced to 12 years of hard labor. The excuse for the severity of the sentence was that probably he was going to be sentenced to death anyway. In 1961, I fled the country by boat, arriving at the Cayman Islands some 44 hours later. After 38 days on the island of Grand Cayman, I arrived in the USA and went to New York to live with my aunt.

I soon settled in and found work. I discovered someone who was practicing Santería and started visiting and worshiping with them. In 1967, I moved to California and was surprised to learn that Santería was being practiced very openly in the Los Angeles area due to the arrival of thousands of Cuban exiles.

After divorcing and losing most of my savings (you have to pay for everything that is done for you in Santería, from a simple reading to any other help), I fell away from worshiping in Santería and started visiting with my daughter at a Foursquare church. However, my house remained full of idols and representations of different *orishas*.

A year later in 1986, a friend invited me to a Full Gospel Businessmen's Fellowship dinner. When I heard the testimony of a member, the Lord touched me and I accepted Jesus as my Savior. This friend was attending Lake Avenue Church in Pasadena and the Sunday School class known as the 120 Fellowship. The teacher was Dr. C. Peter Wagner. Today I am still a member of this same church and the same class. I thank the Lord for taking me there. I believe that I am a Christian today because of the love, compassion, and ministry that the members of the class showed to me.

Roger Nelson, a member of the class, put me in contact with a pastor from Utah. At that time he was one of the very few Christian pastors with a deliverance ministry. He graciously came to my apartment with Roger and prayed deliverance over my daughter and me.

My first two years as a Christian were very difficult, full of guilt and remorse for all that I had done. I still had difficulty accepting forgiveness from the Lord and the concept of being saved and forgiven by grace was still foreign to me.

The support, understanding, and prayers of my sisters and brothers from the Sunday school class were so wonderful that only God could have moved them to so much sacrifice. At that time we were studying the book of Acts in the 120 Fellowship, and I understood what our teacher, Peter Wagner, was explaining. It was a wonderful awakening to walk through this book and to have my daily readings from the Word of God, although I still did not fully understand what I was reading.

Two years later, during our class annual retreat, the Holy Spirit touched me and brought me to a total confession in front of my class.  Tom White, who was leading this retreat, prayed over me and something broke.  My cycle of learning and understanding the Word of God started.  Since then, when reading through the Old Testament every year, the Lord brings back memories of Santería ceremonies and I keep discovering more about how deceiving this cult really is.

## The Counterfeits of Santería

The devil often counterfeits the things of God.  Let's compare the Santería initiation ceremonies to those given to Moses for the priesthood.

"Make sacred garments for your brother Aaron, to give him dignity and honor.  Tell all the skilled men to whom I have given wisdom in such matters that they are to make garments for Aaron, for his consecration, so he may serve me as priest " (Ex. 28:2-3).

In Santería, special garments are made for the different steps of the initiation.  During the first year the devotee has to dress in white; and since the head is shaved during the initiation, his/her head has to be covered for the first three months.

"These are the garments they are to make:  a breast piece, an ephod, a robe, a woven tunic, a turban and a sash.  They are to make these sacred garments for your brother Aaron and his sons, so they may serve me as priests.  Have them use gold, and blue, purple, and scarlet yarn, and fine linen. Make the ephod of gold, and of blue, purple, and scarlet yarn, and of finely twisted linen— the work of a skilled craftsman.  It is to have two shoulder pieces attached to two of its corners, so it can be fastened.  Its skillfully woven waistband is to be like it—of one piece with the ephod and made with gold, and with blue, purple, and scarlet yarn, and with finely twisted linen" (Ex. 28:4-8).

As in this passage of the Bible, where the garments are carefully described, so Santería has specific clothes for each one of the masters (which are demons) to which each devotee will be dedicated.

"This is what you are to do to consecrate them, so they may serve me as priests: Take a young bull and two rams without defect. And from fine wheat flour, without yeast, make bread, and cakes mixed with oil, and wafers spread with oil. Put them in a basket and present them in it—along with the bull and the two rams" (Ex. 29:1-3).

The bull is offered just for those that are initiated as *babalawo* (the higher position); but for the other positions, *orishas* receive offerings of lambs, goats, roosters, hens, doves, and dogs.

"Then bring Aaron and his sons to the entrance to the Tent of Meeting and wash them with water" (Ex. 29:4).

"Take the garments and dress Aaron with the tunic, the robe of the ephod, the ephod itself and the breastpiece. Fasten the ephod on him by its skillfully woven waistband. Put the turban on his head and attach the sacred diadem to the turban. Take the anointing oil and anoint him by pouring it on his head" (Ex. 29:5-7).

In the Santería ceremony, the devotee is brought to the entrance of the place where the ceremony is going to take place. The person is then washed and dressed with their special garments. The difference is that the devotee is blindfolded.

Following the cleansing bath is the ceremony of dedication; and the devotee, with eyes closed, is dedicated to each *orisha* in general, and specifically to the one that will "govern" his or her life. All chants are in *Yoruba*, an African dialect. The devotee never knows what he is agreeing blindly and faithfully to do.

When the secret ceremony ends, the devotees will open their eyes and, lying face down to the floor, will bow first to the altar where all the stones and shells that represent the *orishas* are, then in the same manner will bow to each of the *santeros* that participated in the ceremony. Then the sacrifices start.

Let's examine Satan's counterfeit as we read the following Scriptures:

"Take one of the rams, and Aaron and his sons shall lay their hands on its head. Slaughter it and take the blood and sprinkle it against the altar on all sides. Cut the ram into pieces and wash the inner parts and the legs, putting them with the head and the other pieces" (Ex. 29:15-17).

"Slaughter it, take some of its blood and put it on the lobes of the right ears of Aaron and his sons, on the thumbs of their right hands, and on the big toes of their right feet. Then sprinkle blood against the altar on all sides" (Ex. 20:20).

"And take some of the blood on the altar and some of the anointing oil and sprinkle it on Aaron and his garments and on his sons and their garments. Then he and his sons and their garments will be consecrated" (Ex. 29:21).

In the Santería ceremony, the animals are presented to the devotee, who places his or her forehead to the forehead of the animal. They next touch their shoulder with the head of the animal; then the animal is slaughtered. The blood is poured into bowls that contain the shells and stones representing the *orishas*. Each *orisha* has its own bowl and specific animals are sacrificed to it. The *santero*, who represents the devotee, wets his index finger in the bowl and touches the forehead, behind the ears, the hands, and the feet of the devotee. While doing this, a prayer in *Yoruba* is being said.

"Take from this ram the fat, the fat tail, the fat around the inner parts, the covering of the liver, both kidneys with the fat on them, and the right thigh. (This is the ram for the ordination.)

From the basket of bread made without yeast, which is before the LORD, take a loaf, and a cake made with oil, and a wafer. Put all these in the hands of Aaron and his sons and wave them before the LORD as a wave offering. Then take them from their hands and burn them on the altar along with the burnt offering for a pleasing aroma to the LORD, an offering made to the LORD by fire" (Ex. 29:22-25).

After the sacrificed animals are cleaned, the fat of the tail, the fat around the inner parts, the liver, heart, kidneys, and the left and right thighs are given to the devotee and presented at the altar; along with a basket of bread.

"After you take the breast of the ram for Aaron's ordination, wave it before the LORD as a wave offering, and it will be your share" (Ex. 29:26).

After the sacrifices, food is prepared for the big celebration that takes place the third day after the ordination. At this time, all the *santeros*, families, and friends are invited to feast. The portion given to the *santero* is not only part of the animals but a sum of money that has been agreed upon before hand. Today this amount is usually from $5,000 to $15,000.

The animals for the offering are brought into the ceremony room. The devotee lays his or her hands on the head of the animal as the priest prays in *Yoruba*. Once again, the devotees do not know what is being said nor the commitments they are making, but they agree with all that is said. The animals are slaughtered in the presence of all the idols that the person is going to receive.

Then the altar ("throne" as it is called) is sprinkled with blood, and the initiate is anointed with blood on both the forehead and the big toe. The animals are cooked and the initiate has to eat the food in the company of the other priests who participated in the ceremony.

As we have seen, the biblical ceremonies and those in Santería are very similar; paralleling, imitating.  God directed the former by His holy Word, and Satan counterfeited the Santería ceremony like a copy cat.  I believe that when this ceremony is performed, it makes Satan very happy, because he desperately desires to be worshiped instead of God.

I made this comparison for you to see the deception that is practiced.  There is a great difference between going to have your fortune read, with the accompanying simple payment, and going to ask for help for a personal situation and becoming an initiate to help resolve the personal problem.  It is a very serious thing to ask information or help of priests of Santería because the whole system is built on satanic lies designed to imitate God's system, and lead the requester deep into bondage.

I was a priestess for many years (even though I never sponsored anyone for initiation).  From the moment a person sits across a table in order for a *santero* to read the shells, that person is inviting in and asking for a master who is not Jesus.  They can't understand the prayers that are being prayed by the *santero* in the Yoruba dialect, but they are accepting and promising to follow, obey, and comply with anything the *santero* says.  This leads to total domination of the person by the *orisha* demon working though the *santero*.

They are caught in a trap from which there seems no escape, and no other choice.

## Ministering Deliverance

When ministering deliverance to someone who has been involved in Santería, I always ask how deep was their involvement.  If they have gone once just for a reading, I make sure that they confess, renounce their promises, and ask forgiveness for accepting a master who is not Jesus.

If they have been deeply involved, I break any spirit of control, submission, dependency, lust, homosexuality (this cult is full of homosexuals), slavery, poverty, financial loss, broken families, divorce, loneliness, and abandonment. Then I have them destroy all objects from ceremonies they have kept.

You may ask, *why so much?*  Because devotees accept all of this when they answer "yes" to domination by the *orisha* demon working through the *santero*.  All the prayers may be in a dialect that they do not understand.  Nevertheless, they are promising all of their life, family, finances, and faithfulness to the demonic *orisha*. We shouldn't be surprised, because this is the kind of worship and obeisance that Satan demands from his followers.

At the beginning of involvement, the devotee may begin to prosper.  But as they get deeper into the ceremonies, they "grow" within the scale of authority.  As they are initiated into higher positions, the ceremonies, and the "help," become more and more expensive.

Eventually they start spending all their finances on sessions with the *santero*.  When they have lost almost everything, they find themselves with more needs to resolve, but no more money to pay for ceremonies or readings.  And then they find out that no money means no "help."

The trap becomes deep and dark.  This was my case, and the case of so many of the followers that I knew at the time.  They lost their businesses, their good jobs, and those dealing with drugs were apprehended and taken to jail.  The favor of the *orishas* lasts only as long as the money flows.

# Escaping Santería

To get out of Santería, it doesn't matter if the one involved just went to get a reading, or advanced to different levels of initiation, there are three simple steps to follow:

1.  Make sure that they confess their involvement in ungodly ceremonies, renounce their promises to *orishas*, and ask forgiveness for accepting a master who is not Jesus.

2.  They should get rid of any objects connected with their participation.  If they have been given a piece of jewelry (an object that has been consecrated in a ceremony with a blood sacrifice), either destroy it or take the object to a jeweler, have it melted down, and designed as something else.  It is necessary to destroy with fire the sacrificial dedication.  If they have received "*collares*" (necklaces), just cut them up and throw them in the garbage.  As to shells, smash them with a hammer until they are broken and throw them away.  Porcelain objects also must be smashed.  Metal objects should be placed into a safe container and burned using rags and charcoal fluid or paint thinner if necessary.  Light and burn the material.  When cool, throw the remains into the garbage.  (Under no circumstances should they return anything to the *santero* who gave it to them.)

3.  They need to seek deliverance with a ministry that knows about witchcraft.  They will need to learn how to stand against the attack of the enemy because they will probably need to, trust me.  Their health and finances will be the

primary target, but if they trust the Lord, they will be victorious.

The morning after I accepted Jesus as my Lord and Savior, I disposed of all that I had received during 20 years of priesthood. Within a week, they (*santeros*) sent someone to tell me that the *orishas* (idols) spoke in the previous night's ceremony saying that I would be dead in three months. But I believed that Jesus was stronger. I accepted Jesus in March of 1983, and I'm still alive! The power of the Holy Spirit is certainly far greater than that of our enemy.

I praise the Lord and thank Him for His forgiveness, deliverance, and healing (not only of my body but of the wounds of my soul from childhood to adulthood as well). I have no words to describe the freedom, especially the peace, that Jesus has brought into my life. I daily enjoy His peace and presence. I am so grateful that He delivered me from the satanic religion of Santería.

Because of His great mercy, He has chosen me to help others also find His freedom and peace. I now have the great privilege to lead a ministry of personal deliverance called Fountain of Freedom Ministries. Praise God for His everlasting faithfulness!

# Chapter Five

# There's Nothing New About New Age

## Chris Hayward

Chris Hayward's call to ministry came in 1983 when he was ordained and served as associate pastor of a spirit-filled Baptist Church in Waco, Texas. Chris then served for 10 years as the first senior pastor with Christian Fellowship Church in Mt. Vernon, Illinois. In 1994 Cleansing Stream Ministries (CSM) was introduced to the church, and, beginning with a small group, it eventually ministered to over 90% of the congregation. In June, 1998 he resigned the pastorate to become the Executive Director of CSM. Chris and his wife, Karen, were married in 1970 and have three children. To learn more about Cleansing Stream Ministries, please call 800-580-8190 or visit www.cleansingstream.org.

I was fourteen years old and spiritually hungry. Our family had left Canada for California only three years earlier. Our stay in Canada was an unplanned, four-year stopover after leaving our homeland of England. My parents had joined a Community Church in Lakewood. For me it was a spiritual wasteland. While it possessed all the markings of a "house of the Lord," it had none of its characteristics (although I must admit, I would not have been able to identify truth from error at this point in my life).

All I knew was that there was more to life than the "natural" universe. I was on a search, but I could not tell you exactly what I was searching *for*. I wanted something or someone to explain why I was here – and if there was a purpose to my existence. In church I sang hymns and listened to sermons that seemed to have no relevance. The Word of God was unknown to me and disregarded by the pastor and his followers. So, I began my quest to obtain some meaning to life. I began to read everything available about spirituality.

Looking back I can tell you that in the absence of truth, the spirit of error will find a way to captivate the "open-minded." My mind was open, and the enemy of my soul purposed to fill it with whatever would lure me away from God.

Standing in the wings of every yearning soul is the kingdom of darkness. Like a vulture circling its prey, it is ready and willing to devour those to whom the church should be reaching out. In the absence of truth, lies will flourish. I bought into these lies with great abandon. What I embraced was everything that is espoused by New Age. Of course, at that time, 1960, the term "New Age" had not yet been popularized.

## What is Meant by "New Age"?

"New Age" is actually a catchall phrase. This term was first made popular by Alice Bailey, the founder of an offshoot of the Theosophical Society (which began in New York in 1875 by the Russian-born occultist, H. P. Blavatsky) in the 1930s. In 1960 it again became popular by Baba Ram Dass (alias Richard Alpert) and others as it became identified with the coming "Age of Aquarius." It was said that humanity would finally "come of age." Such ideas as "new world order," "peace and harmony," "higher or cosmic consciousness," and "universal love" became popular.

There was a rejection of materialism and science. Institutions that seemed to have no relevance to the meaning of life, or exhibited nothing of power or fulfillment were rejected. Unfortunately, Christianity seemed to fall into that category ("having a form of godliness but lacking the power thereof," 2 Tim. 3:5).

In the midst of such a void many became attracted to spiritualism and the Theosophical Society. Soon there were many offshoots. Drawn into the vortex were Christian mystics, Jewish Cabalists, and previously obscure Christian heretics. Gurus appeared from the East. Zen Buddhism and Sufism gained much interest, which prepared the ground for the Dalai Lama. Parapsychology flourished, along with channeling, mediums, Paganism, and Wicca (witchcraft). England alone purports to have over 20,000 witches.

## The Core of New Age

At the core of New Age are the beliefs of reincarnation, evolutionary thinking, self-realization, self-improvement, or spiritual healing (this form of spiritual healing cannot be confused with the Christian approach of dependence upon the Holy Spirit). Many of these found their way into major corporations by which they sought to assist their key personnel to become motivated and fulfilled. Other avenues of thinking that are greatly embraced are matriarchal forms of religious thinking such as the "Mother-Goddess" and a female priesthood. Even much of the interest in extraterrestrial beings has its roots in New Age thinking. So-called "encounters of the third kind" always seem to accompany New Age philosophies and doctrine.

Sir George Trevelyan is a well-know English leader of the New Age movement. He is the founder of the Wrekin Trust, a New Age center. He sums up his New Age worldview in *A Vision of the Aquarian Age* (Coventure, 1977):

"Behind all outwardly manifested form is a timeless realm of absolute consciousness. It is the great Oneness underlying all the diversity, all the myriad forms of nature. It may be called God, or may be deemed beyond all naming.... The world of nature, in short, is but a reflection of the eternal world of Creative imagining. The inner core of man, that which in each of us might be called spirit, is a droplet of the divine source. As such, it is imperishable and eternal, for life cannot be extinguished. The outer sheath in which it manifests can, of course, wear out and be discarded; but to speak of 'death' in relation to the true being and spirit of man is irrelevant" (pp. 5-6).

Strongly suggested here is the most popular belief within the New Age movement – reincarnation.  Sir George further states:

"The soul belongs properly to higher and purer spheres.  It incarnates for the purpose of acquiring experience in the density of earth matter – a necessary educational phase in its development. Such incarnation, of course, entails drastic limitation of a free spiritual being.  Birth into a body is, in fact, more like entry into a species of tomb" (p.6).  He explains his reasoning as follows: "More precisely, we must recognize man as a threefold being of body, soul and spirit.... The immortal 'I' is neither the soul nor the transient personality.  In order to descend into the density of the phenomenal world, it must clothe itself, so to speak, in a protective sheath.  The 'soul' is therefore the sheath or 'astral body,' which the eternal 'I' draws about it in order to experience the psychological level of reality.  (It also draws around itself an 'atheric' body of vital forces to hold together the physical body.)"

To the average Christian this sounds like a lot of hogwash. But to those outside of Christ seeking something that sounds steeped with meaning, it can become appealing.  Something to note is the blatant disregard for the correct use of spirit, soul, and body.  The New Ager is especially adept at nodding in agreement with your words while all along redefining what they mean.

## A Personal Quest for Identity and Ability

Let me give you an example.  In 1964, I joined the Army.  My basic training took place at Ft. Polk, Louisiana.  After that, I received specialized training at Ft. Benjamin Franklin in Indianapolis, Indiana. I was trained as a personnel specialist. Within a few weeks, my orders sent me to White Sands Missile Range, New Mexico. My basic duties were simple enough, and I was enjoying other activities as well. I had begun flight training prior to joining the Army and found a way to continue it at White Sands. I also landed a job at the base pool as a lifeguard during the summer months.

Life was pretty good – until I received new orders. It seemed that I was about to be transferred to an outpost in the middle of the desert away from all my enjoyable activities. I couldn't allow this to happen. As a matter of policy, the base chaplain would conduct an orientation meeting for all new personnel. He explained that he was in need of a Chaplain's Assistant. I felt that I could fool him with enough spiritual lingo to convince him I would make an excellent assistant and have my orders changed.

He was convinced of my spirituality (so much for discernment), and then convinced the general to have my orders changed. When questioned about my faith in Christ, I simply converted the terminology to my own understanding. I knew the intent of the questioner, but simply justified my response on the basis of my "superior understanding." Such pride is commonplace among New Age devotees.

The reason for this is quite simple – and understanding why enables us to share our faith effectively. Those caught up in New Age teaching have an insatiable appetite for personal identity. *They want to know for what purpose they were born, and they want to display power.* Those who are articulate, exhibiting personal confidence, and claiming to possess particular powers, have an immediate following. Consequently, the observer is on a personal quest for identity and ability. I found that whenever I was around others in this field, there was an underlying pressure to impress them with what I knew or could do. Of course the hunger for identity is remedied in the foundation of the gospel:

"For God so loved the world that He gave His only begotten Son, that whoever believes in Him should not perish but have everlasting life" (John 3:16).

It is further emphasized throughout the first chapter of Ephesians beginning with:

"Blessed be the God and Father of our Lord Jesus Christ, who has blessed us with every spiritual blessing in the heavenly places in Christ..." (Eph. 1:3).

As someone involved in the New Age, I had a counterfeit term for just about every biblical term or phrase. Jesus Christ was savior, inasmuch as He came to enlighten those who were less spiritually aware. He was a master of the highest plane, having gone through the required reincarnations. Though not God, He was godlike, but not totally unique. There were other "masters." If you spoke about Christ, I would automatically think about "Christ-consciousness," the higher plain of understanding, which enveloped and influenced the "enlightened."

## New Age Understanding of Christ

I was proud and arrogant and absolutely convinced that I was right. I would have died for what I believed. It is hard to convince someone like that – especially when they will patronize you if you attempt to witness to them. They'll nod kindly as you speak, assessing you as simply an immature child in your spiritual growth – thinking that you still have many more reincarnations to go through before you would perhaps understand the deeper truths.

The god worshiped by those in New Age is themselves. Christ is seen as being within each and every person, though not perhaps recognized.  To many New Age authors, "the Christ" who spoke through Jesus of Nazareth was the highest of true teachers.  In a work called *Esoteric Christianity* (Theosophical Publishing Society, 1905), Annie Besant writes: "The historical Christ, then, is a glorious Being belonging to the great spiritual hierarchy that guides the spiritual evolution of humanity, who used for some three years the human body of the disciple Jesus,...who drew men to Him by

> # Looking back I can tell you that in the absence of truth, the spirit of error will find a way to captivate the "open-minded."

the singular love and tenderness, and the rich wisdom that breathed from His Person; and who was finally put to death for blasphemy, for teaching the inherent Divinity of Himself and of all men" (pp. 140-141).

They very simply have not read nor understood the Gospel of John in which is stated:

"In the beginning was the Word, and the Word was with God, and the Word was God.  He was in the beginning with God.  All things were made through Him, and without Him nothing was made that was made.  In Him was life, and the life was the light of men" (John 1:1-4).

## How Should Christians Respond?

New Age teachers think nothing of reinventing the Scriptures.  Very few of them have even read the Word of God.  Most have read a little and taken the meanings out of context, or have taken what they believe it says and twisted it out of proportion. Those who read their writings know even less. It is a fundamental fact that although they purport to be open-minded, they are most definitely close-minded to historic Christianity.

As Christians we can respond in one of two ways. We can denounce such activity as being abhorrent to God and the followers destined for the eternal flames, or we can acknowledge the failure of the church to recognize a legitimate hunger in the lives of searching souls. Rather than looking askance at its followers, we can use this growing interest as a platform for evangelism.

The hunger is to know the meaning of life, true power, and to experience love in its deepest form. No one has the answer to these, other than God's people. Jesus Christ, raised from the dead by the power of the Holy Spirit, Who is now given to us, that we might know the width, the length, the height, and the depth of God's love, is the answer. He alone can satisfy the longing of the New Ager.

The gospel demonstrated with power will place the New Age where it belongs – in the shadows of darkness. Why would anyone want to hug and kiss a shadow, if the real can be embraced?

There is nothing new about New Age. It can be found in the declarations of prohibited activities listed in Deuteronomy 18:

"There shall not be found among you anyone who makes his son or his daughter pass through the fire, or one who practices witchcraft, or a soothsayer, or one who interprets omens, or a sorcerer, or one who conjures spells, or a medium, or a spiritist, or one who calls up the dead" (vv. 10-11).

It will always surface with new names – but under the skin it is still the same. We must love the New Ager and not denounce them for searching for truth. Our challenge is to place the true light on Jesus, the lover of their souls.

## My Emergence

I would like to end this chapter by sharing with you how I came to leave all this for Jesus Christ. Perhaps it will provide some understanding as to how we might help those caught up in New Age philosophy.

The last eighteen months of my Army duty was spent in Vietnam (1967-68). Near the end of my duty there I found myself in the home of a missionary. Paul Travis and his wife had been in Vietnam for over 42 years. They had been through the Japanese occupation, the French occupation, and now the American occupation of this small but strategic country.

This godly couple had been instrumental in establishing a number of churches throughout the land. He was highly respected, and I was grossly ignorant. I was a chaplain's assistant – and still as lost as a rock. Since the age of fourteen, my life's ambition was wrapped up in the occult, to become a medium. Being fairly well versed, I gave a lesson to Mr. Travis, thinking he could learn from my vast experience and knowledge.

For almost thirty minutes, he somehow endured my endless nonsense. I sat on his counter while he cut vegetables in his little home in Qui Nyon. He was getting a lesson on reincarnation, the necessity of karma, and spiritism. I was teaching him all about the great teachers and thinkers of our time. Finally he'd had enough. He put known his knife, looked at me and said, "What a shame!" Shocked, I replied, "What do you mean, 'What a shame!'?" He simply responded, "You don't believe in a personal God, do you?" With one simple remark I was undone. No Scripture, no sermon – just one simple question.

For two weeks his words rocked me. All my life I had been yearning to know God. I knew there had to be something or Someone. From that moment of reckoning, I had felt like a bucket full of holes, and whatever I tried to fill it with quickly flowed out. The security of feeling like I had everything figured out evaporated. My head and my heart were corrupt, and I was empty inside.

Now sitting on a sandbag wall around the perimeter of the 504th Military Police Battalion where I was assigned, I was at the end of myself. Despite my extensive pursuit of spirituality, I had never spoken with God before. A sandbag became my altar.

My prayers, up to that time had been all about myself, and I had done the talking. Now, God had something to say to me. In the presence of His infinite holiness, a mirror was put up to my life. All the ugliness and façade was there. My belief system was empty – it just wouldn't hold up under the strain of this life.

God gave me a choice that night: I was invited to embrace His Son, Jesus Christ, or choose to forever walk the path I currently traveled. I recall running into the chapel tent, falling on my knees and crying out, "Jesus, Jesus." At the time, that was the depth of my theological understanding. But it was sufficient – for "whoever calls on the name of the LORD shall be saved" (Romans 10:13). I needed Jesus, and He came in. Then my Christian walk began. It took some time for much of the erroneous false New Age teachings to fall off. But in time, and through the Word, they were quickly replaced.

There is hope for those entrapped by New Age thinking. With a loving approach, explaining that they can really know the love of God in a personal way, and through much prayer, they can be won for Christ.

# Chapter Six

# Rescued from Satanism

## Jeff Harshbarger

Jeff Harshbarger, along with his wife Liz, established the work of Refuge Ministries in order to help those that have been involved in Satanism, the occult, Wicca and witchcraft, New Age and false teachings in the Christian church.

Jeff was delivered from Satanism by the power of Jesus Christ in 1981. He holds a M.A. in Pastoral Counseling and travels all over the world sharing what Jesus Christ has done for him and teaching on the topic of Deliverance. For further information go to www.refugeministries.cc.

*"I shall not die, but live,*
*and declare the works of the Lord."*
*Psalm 118:17*

I grew up in a military family. We moved a lot, and I mean a lot. Between the ages of 6-12, we moved 5 times. This type of lifestyle makes it very difficult for a child to have friends and establish any kind of positive roots.

My father came back from the Viet Nam war a very different person than when he had left. He left when I was a baby, which caused us not to bond. He returned very angry and began to drink heavily. This resulted in violence becoming a normal part of our family life. My parents fought and I was physically and verbally abused. And as we moved from small town to small town, I felt the shame of being the town drunks' kid.

## My First Encounter with Jesus Christ

I was not doing very well in school by the third grade because the violence and abuse had taken its toll. When I did go to school, I would just want to cry. To sit in a classroom full of "normal" kids and to perform, was just too much to expect of me. I began to see a school therapist. And, I started to notice that I was becoming as angry as my father was.

It was during this time that I began to notice something about my life. It was something that was unexplainable. There were times when I would get up to go to the bathroom or to get a drink of water and I would feel a presence in my house. I didn't know what I was experiencing, but it was like something – or someone – was aware of me and following me around. I wasn't fearful of the experience, though I simply did not know what to think.

Curiosity began to cause me to get up more frequently, just to see if the presence would be there. And it was. As this continued, I became more and more curious.

Near the end of the school year, I was invited to attend Vacation Bible School. I wasn't too excited about the idea, but my mother found out about it, and made sure that I attended the first day. Once I was there, I liked it. We had crafts, we ate cookies, and we had a story about Jesus. It didn't take long before I wanted to know this Man by the Name of Jesus. I accepted Him as my Savior and would pray to Him. I was given a Bible, but I did not know how to read it. It was very confusing to me. So, my relationship with Him was through prayer. I went to church on my own for a short time, because my family wasn't attending. And, when I did go to church, I just didn't connect with the church, or I wasn't being followed-up on. So, I quit going to church, but I would pray to Him before I went to sleep.

## Seeking in the Dark

I was in my bedroom one night by myself playing with Ouija Board and had the shock of my life! Thinking that this was just simply a game, I took the pointer and I began to ask the board questions. To my amazement the oracle moved by itself! I was scared to death, but I was thrilled at the reality of this happening. I knew at this point that there was a "power" behind what I had just experienced. And it immediately reminded me of my previous experience of a presence that was in my house. What was I on to? I had a million questions and I wanted to know more.

With the desire to know more about the power behind the Ouija Board and about the presence that I had experienced in my house, I opened the door for the supernatural to become a common occurrence. I had an incredible experience when I astral-projected into a house which we were going to move into.

I began to be able to see things before they happened in dreams. For example, I had a dream that I saw through the wrapping on a Christmas gift. I knew what was in the present before I opened it! This just kept feeding my desire for more until I got to a point of experiencing the presence of demons and supernatural abilities. I was very excited about all of this and began to pull away from my family and live in my own little world.

## My Descent into Satanism

By high school, I was done with Jesus Christ. I had attempted to go to church, but it just wasn't working out for me. I had many supernatural experiences and I wanted to pursue finding out more about it. I was very aware of the media's coverage of Jeanne Dixon and Uri Gellar and I thought that I possessed the same abilities as they did. Maybe I was a clairvoyant or had psychic abilities.

It was during this time that my parents finally divorced. I thought that the divorce would bring a level of peace to our home situation. At least there would not be anymore fighting. But the divorce only caused further isolation among the family members. My resolve was that I was going to pursue the abilities that I possessed. I was actually hoping that I could fine-tune my clairvoyant or psychic abilities and make a living at it.

My mother received Jesus Christ as her Lord and Savior soon after her divorce and our household environment changed. She began to attend church and bothered me ferociously to attend, as well. I really wasn't interested, though. She constantly played Christian music or television. She was having prayer in the kitchen with her friend before I would get out of bed for school. This was too much for me. I pulled away. I even watched a Christian show and said to the Lord that I wanted no part of Him.

I soon took a job at the local department store and met the man who would "evangelize" me and eventually lead me to Satanism. He was the associate manger of the store and I found him to be very charismatic. He had an ability about him that I admired. I found myself wanting whatever he had to offer.

The offer to become a Satanist came one evening as I was working and we had a snowfall that paralyzed my hometown. There was no way for me to get home and the associate manager asked if I would like to stay in his apartment. I immediately took him up on his offer. When I went to his place, I recognized that he had the same presence in his apartment that I experienced as a child. I was intrigued! I began to discuss with him the things of the supernatural and he took over the conversation, which led to his invitation to become a Satanist. I accepted and was filled with an unholy spirit that evening through a satanic initiation ritual.

## My Life as a Satanist

I immediately recognized a change after the night of my initiation. Within a very short time, I went from being a fearful, wallflower type personality to possessing a bold, commanding presence. I dressed for success and I knew that the earth was mine because I served the god of this world. We had a covenant; I would exchange my soul for his power and abilities.

It was my responsibility to offer myself to my new god as a living sacrifice and to be filled with his presence. I was to die to my nature, in that I was to die to what is human. I was to give over to Satan my need for love and in exchange he would give me power. My heart was to die. This was the ultimate sacrifice of my call to be a Satanist.

I began my walk in Satanism as a "religious" or "philosophical" Satanist. This type of Satanism is referred to as modern Satanism and does not adhere to the belief in a real Satan. It holds to a "satanic" philosophy, or self-deification through indulgence. The "scripture" for this ideology is the satanic Bible written by Anton Szandor LaVey. He began the move of modern

## There was the presence of a Being more powerful than I had ever met in all my years as a Satanist.

Satanism in San Francisco in 1966. Because there are rituals and a belief system that this type of Satanism promotes, it is termed "religious" Satanism.

However, I was soon confounded in my walk as a Satanist and began to change my perspective and practice from that of a "philosophical" Satanist to a traditional Satanist. This type of Satanism accepts the reality of Satan and demons. It is, in essence, devil worship. The basis of this type of Satanism was the exchange of one's soul through possession for demonic power.

I did not succeed in my Satanism. After several years as a Satanist, I came to a place where my heart was not dying and my growth was hampered. I was told by my satanic mentor that I could not grow as a Satanist because I was "angelically oppressed." I had been, up to this point, serving the most powerful being I knew of. And yet, I was being told that there was a power that was stronger than what I was possessed by. I had to find out what this Higher Power was. And when I recognized that the Higher Power was Jesus Christ, I wanted no part of Him. I had been conditioned to hate the Name of Jesus Christ.

Everything that I had put my hope and heart into had failed me. I was being tormented by the absence of meaning and purpose. I had received no answers to the questions that I had in my life.

The demons that I had invited to possess me soon began to torment me. We were no longer walking in covenant and they were looking to destroy me. It was at this point that I attempted suicide twice. I wanted to die.

Death would come easily, or so I thought. I purchased my gun, took the usual means of sedating my fears – marijuana and whiskey – and headed for the place to finalize my ruin. I checked into a hotel room and smoked and drank myself to a place where I would have the nerve to pull the trigger. I would probably make the evening news. But as I sat there, I began to wrestle with the thought of this being the end.

When I put the barrel to my head, fear came to me. I wasn't afraid to die. I was afraid of where I would go after I died. So I didn't, or rather couldn't, pull the trigger. Again, I felt the failure of my life, even in my death.

With the realization of my desire to die being still unfulfilled, I attempted to destroy myself again the next afternoon. I took a rope and attempted to hang myself. I tied the rope over the garage rafter.

I made sure that the knot was nice and tight as I tied the other end around my neck. I felt as though I was ready. My issue with my eternal destiny was meaningless at this point.

I kicked the chair out from under my feet expecting to experience the jerk of the rope on my neck. I found myself on the floor of my garage instead. I sat there wondering why I was not dead. How could I fail, again?

I was miserable. I had failed at suicide twice. Not only had I desired to die, I failed twice in fulfilling that desire. Was there a way out? What could or should I do at this point? I found myself with a million new questions. Where would I go to find the answers? I needed a beer.

That evening, after failing at suicide for the second time, I thought I would try to drink myself into a stupor. However, I couldn't. Every time that I would attempt to draw the beer can to my lips, the smell of the alcohol would nauseate me. This was highly unusual. I had been a drinker for years.

I attempted to light a cigarette, but it would burn my lips and the smell was as bad as the beer. I attempted to smoke some marijuana in order to get a high that might curb my pain. But, just like the beer, the smell of the joint was nauseating. Nothing could sedate my condition. My old friends, alcohol and drugs, were suddenly inconsumable. I couldn't even smoke a cigarette. I was confused.

I went outside to clear my head. However, the questions were too strong. I couldn't die and I was not in my planned drunken stupor. I didn't want to feel what I was feeling, at that point. I was unable to take my life and I did not know what to do.

Sleep was the only way to relieve my pain and confusion. I fell onto my bed seeking to close my eyes. As I lay there, I began to cry. All the years of my seeking answers had produced nothing. I had such a strong desire to die and yet, I failed at this two times. Failure. All I felt was failure.

As I began to cry, I felt a tremendous relief in my tears. However, as I wept, I experienced something that I had not before. I heard a voice from the foot of my bed, demanding "Get out!"

I immediately quit crying, expecting to see a demon appear in order to destroy me. I had attempted to kill myself and thought that I had angered the demonic host by my attempt to take my life.

Again the voice insisted "Get out!" However, this time I heard the voice from right beside my face. I did not hesitate to respond to what I was told. I got out of the room and went outside of my house. I actually stepped through my bedroom window so as to not waste a moment getting out of where I was.

When I stepped outside, I experienced the presence of God. There was the presence of a Being more powerful than I had ever met in all my years as a Satanist. But, I somehow knew that this Being cared for me.

I fell on my face and began to weep. As I raised my head from my driveway, I asked Jesus Christ to make my life okay. I knew Who I was meeting. I knew at that moment that I was in the presence of Jesus Christ and I just wanted Him to make my life okay.

I wasn't conscious of accepting Him as my Lord and Savior at that moment. I just needed to make it through that time in my life. I thought that I would only ask Him to help me. And He did. The same Jesus Christ that I had walked away from numerous times spoke to me in my despair.

## A Very Present Help in Time of Need

Jesus Christ led me out of Satanism and led me to a small church for the help that I was so greatly in need of. I sat in the back row of a small church in Muncie, Indiana in 1981, and listened to the first sermon of my life. It was after that service that a man approached me by the name of Harry Richardson. He asked me over to dinner at his and his wife's home. I gladly accepted the invitation.

I sat down with Harry and Jo Richardson for dinner and for a night that would change my life. To this point, I still had the demons inside me and they were still tormenting me. As I sat there I was not sure how this evening was going to turn out. It went well. We talked in order to get to know one another, even though it was somewhat awkward. But soon, I was sharing with them that I had been involved in Satanism. Jo told me that I was in need of prayer. She began to pray and I was delivered from the demons that had been tormenting me.

I immediately experienced a change when I knew they were gone. I ran to the nearest mirror and looked at the reflection of my real self for the first time in years. I had been used to seeing the demons in me ever since I was initiated. It was good to see only me, and I smiled for the first time in years!

It was through Harry and Jo Richardson that I received the help to be delivered from the demons and the effects of my involvement in Satanism. They offered me the love that my heart was seeking, and I was counseled and discipled in the Word of God. I thank God that He led me to individuals who knew how to be used by Him in the area of deliverance.

There is a way out of Satanism. I was so glad when I found that way. The Bible is true when it says Jesus is the way, the truth, and the life (John 14:6). I will forever be grateful for His mercy and love for me.

# Chapter Seven

# Out of the Dark Prison of Voodoo

## Ana Mendez Ferrell

Ana was saved in 1985 while she was confined in a mental hospital after having been a voodoo priestess. The miraculous power of God totally delivered her and transformed her into one of His generals for leading His army to destroy the works of evil. Originally from Mexico, she now resides in Jacksonville, Florida and is married to Emerson Ferrell. Together they head up Voice of the Light Ministries, equipping the body of Christ through training and prayer in 40 nations. She is the author of *Shaking the Heavens*, *High Level Warfare*, and *Seated in Heavenly Places*. To learn more about these and other resources she has made available, please visit anamendez.org or write to Voice of the Light Ministries, PO Box 3418, Ponte Vedra, FL 32004.

It was one of those experiences in life you could never forget – nor stop pondering the significance of, even years later. One evening when I was eighteen years old, I was in my bedroom preparing for a final exam. As I sat studying, something began to distract me. I began feeling a powerful, supernatural force drawing me toward my window.

Despite the cloudy darkness of the night sky, I saw a spectacular bright light shining through. It resembled a gigantic star. As I intently pondered what it could be, the light suddenly broke away, pierced through my window, and filled my room with a dazzling splendor. I fell to the floor unable to move. All I could do was weep before the indescribable love and infinite goodness that surrounded me. This presence caused me to feel filthy and insignificant, yet blessed beyond anything I could have imagined.

Suddenly, I was not able to see any of my surroundings as they were. My eyes only saw the Lord Jesus in all of His majesty! Christ Himself had come to visit with me! I awkwardly wrote down what He spoke to me. I do not know how many hours went by as little by little the vision began to vanish. I found myself on the floor soaked in tears, holding a piece of paper in my hand that said: "I am your Lord, Jesus Christ, and I come to tell you that, in time, I will make Myself known to you. You will be my servant and I will come to you through a man with blue eyes."

From that moment on, I fell deeply in love with Jesus. And I began a desperate search to find God and to serve Him. Having been raised as a Catholic, I started my quest in the Roman Church where I found nothing but emptiness and a ritualistic religion sorely lacking the presence of the supernatural majestic God for which I was looking.

## The Path to the Occult

In Mexico, where I grew up, I never heard of a Christian church. This gave the devil an opportunity to drive me into a horrendous snare and into the paths of the occult. My thirst for a kingdom of invisible power coming from God, my brokenhearted youth, and my ignorance of the ways of the Lord, were the perfect ingredients for Satan to trap my soul.

Disappointed by the powerlessness of Catholicism, I made my way into the Eastern Religions. I wanted to find Jesus no matter what it took. In these philosophies they speak about an "Avatar" called Jesus, an anointed spirit that has visited the earth in the form of Buddha, Krishna, and others. So I gave it a try, in the only way I know how to do things – totally sold out. After two years of yoga and meditation, I realized that the marvelous Jesus who once visited me, was not in that philosophy either. Nevertheless, those practices were the first step the devil used to create a fascination in me for the unknown, for the mysteries of the universe, and for the search of the occult – the ways of the so-called "Great Universal Mind."

Shortly after I left Eastern Religious practices, I was introduced to a man who is best described as a powerful warlock, a shaman, and a master of the occult. He was known as "an enlightened one," one of the few chosen who could enter into the realms of the spirit, and have contact with the gods.

Talking to him was very appealing. He spoke of God, the universe, of magical powers, and of worlds, in a way that left me speechless. As the words came out of his mouth, a seducing spirit captured my soul. I was caught in something so powerful that I wanted to be part of it. He then opened a Bible and read to me John chapter three, and said to me: "you must be born again in order to enter the kingdom of God." This, he explained, is the kingdom of magic where all things are possible. Satan's arrow pierced my soul at that moment, and I fell into the web that drove me into the depths of the kingdom of darkness.

## Into the Prison of Voodoo

A couple of weeks later, I was initiated into voodoo magic, through the traditional "initiatrix death." The initiation ceremony, based mostly on animal sacrifices recorded in the book of Leviticus, called for the one being initiated to be bathed in blood which was supposed to represent atoning blood.

After a series of rituals (described more fully in my book, *High Level Warfare*), I found myself outside of my body, floating in the middle of the room. I watched as a series of demonic beings entered into my body. When my spirit returned to my body, I felt as if a fully charged, high-voltage battery jolted me. After the ceremony drew to a close, I was no longer myself. I was under the power of a force that would guide my steps in the world of the occult. I had been terribly deceived and my soul was now in covenant with the devil.

That is when my work with the warlock began. We did witchcraft, read cards, and initiated others whenever possible. The warlock insisted that we were practicing white magic and that our alliance was only with spirits of light that came from beautiful saints and virgins whose mission was to help us in our daily walk on earth. Little by little I realized this was not true, but the phrase that echoed within me was, "Once you enter into this path, there is no way out."

The spirit voices within me were becoming clearer as time went on. These spirits were powerful and had the ability to heal the sick and perform deliverance (which was deceitful, because we would pull out one spirit only to replace it with another). The person left rejoicing believing they were free, only to have the "cast out" spirit eventually return and take revenge against them.

I walked further and further into the deepest prisons of voodoo magic. I developed a thirst for blood and enjoyed animal sacrifices. The power exuded as they died became like a drug to me. As I grew in knowledge and ascended to different levels of the occult, the devil began manifesting himself just as he was, rather than the beautiful being he had pretended to be in the beginning. I was in tyranny, forced to obey at any price. My home was completely bewitched. I spent endless nights terrorized by spirits assigned to torture me to exhaustion.

On the other hand, I was favored with fame, money, and influential friends. By the time I achieved the level of priestess in voodoo magic, I had the authority to ask for whatever I needed for my works of magic. It was then that I began to notice that there were some things the devil simply could not do. All the power he boasted about had limits. There were places he could not go and people he couldn't touch no matter how many sacrifices or ceremonies we performed. I became very angry with him when I understood he was not able to make good on all his claims of power.

## "You Are Going to Die"

When he realized that I knew the truth about his weaknesses and the limitations of his power, the enemy decided to kill me. This he made clear to me one day when one of his emissaries announced to me: "I come to claim what belongs to me. I am coming for you, your time has come."

That year was filled with horrific, deadly attacks against me. The first came during a war in El Salvador where part of my family lives. I fell seriously ill with pneumonia and needed to be hospitalized. While there, the city was attacked and a bomb exploded right next to the hospital where I was staying. Soon after, while in Los Angeles, two men assaulted me at gunpoint. Their intentions were to rape and kill me, but I now know that God's hand was on me. They beat me up and left me in the street, but strangely nothing further happened. A few months later, the assailants were caught and imprisoned for having killed seven other people in that same neighborhood.

Shortly after the attack, a gas tank in my apartment caught fire. I put it out using a blanket and my body while the devil screamed, "You are going to die." Then, Mexico City's terrible earthquake hit, killing over 300,000 people. My apartment was located in the disaster zone where hundreds of buildings were demolished. While trying to rescue people trapped alive in the rubble, the building exploded and my body was expelled. Even so, the fire did not touch me. I once again experienced God's hand over my life.

The devil's voice became increasingly stronger and more frequent, "I have come for you, you belong to me, and you are going to die." My nerves, along with the demons tormenting me, were destroying me. My health began to fail and I suffered strong nervous breakdowns. I decided to fly to Puerto Rico for a rest, when a torrential storm destroyed a mountain nearby. I, once again, was surrounded by corpses and by those crushed by rubble.

I suffered a partial facial palsy because of my deteriorating psychological condition. I experienced extreme pain in that year and finally understood how the soul becomes anesthetized when suffering reaches its breaking point. The devil took me into the deepest chambers of hell where I saw lost souls beaten and burned to their executioners' joy. I knew the true meaning of the darkness, when life no longer has a single ray of hope – where there is no escape from oppression, loneliness, or sadness.

I went back to Mexico in an attempt to stop the torment, but ended up far from it. The demons that had been tormenting me turned the power against me to kill me once and for all. It was a fierce battle within me that lasted until I, unable to bear it any longer, attempted to take my life by slitting me veins.

I lost a lot of blood by the time my twin sister found me and took me to the hospital. While I was in the emergency room, battling between life and death, the unexpected happened. A glorious presence started descending over me. It was the same light I had seen so many years ago when Jesus first visited me in my room. I then heard an audible voice say to me, "Your Heavenly Father is not going to abandon you." Peace finally embraced me as the strong sedatives that were administered to me took effect.

## Set Free!

I woke up 48 hours later in the psychiatric wing of the hospital – a remote building with security bars and mentally ill patients. I was one of them and still in extremely poor condition. After several medical evaluations, the doctor determined that my prognosis was very serious and I would certainly remain in the hospital

> **At that moment, I felt as if lightning had fallen from heaven braking the chains that held me captive. As the demons fled, joy and peace filled my heart and I was fully convinced that Jesus had totally set me free.**

for a long time. But God's plans were different. Several days later, my beloved aunt Gloria Capriles came to see me. She was a beautiful, sweet lady full of love and compassion. She told me there was a man who had changed her life and she wanted to bring him to see me. I agreed, more out of curiosity than faith.

The next day she walked in with a Christian pastor. His eyes were a striking blue. I listened attentively as he presented the message of salvation. I knew what he was saying was true. Nonetheless, my reaction was to weep bitterly in intense sadness. "This is a terrible thing you are preaching," I told him. "I know everything you are saying is true, but I am unable to run to Jesus. I have made unbreakable covenants and if I try to break them, the devil's wrath will come on me."

In that moment of deep despair, the minister interrupted me by saying, "That's not true! The Word of God says, '*if we confess our sins, He is faithful and just to forgive us our sins and to cleanse us from all unrighteousness.*' The blood of Jesus breaks every covenant! Jesus, our Lord, died for you to deliver you from the devil's chains!"

His words shook me and the Holy Spirit began a deep work in my soul. "What must I do to receive Jesus in my heart," I asked through my tears, with a deep longing for my beloved Jesus to put an end to the nightmare.

"Repent and ask Him to live in your heart. Tell Him you want to make Him your Lord and Savior."

When I did, the Holy Spirit came on me with such conviction of sin that I broke down in a mixture of pain and shame. My conscience was being purged as I poured my soul out to God, begging for mercy. It was during that deep and sincere prayer that God removed the deception and I was able to clearly see how the devil had ensnared me. After a time of confession, the minister prayed for my deliverance from the demons that had held me in their grasp. At that moment, I felt as if lightning had fallen from heaven braking the chains that held me captive. As the demons fled, joy and peace filled my heart and I was fully convinced that Jesus had totally set me free.

## Declaring War

During the days I spent in the hospital, God's presence was extremely powerful in my life. The first thing the Holy Spirit told me was to not even think of turning back in the slightest, because the enemy was furious with me and the decision I had made to follow Christ. Far from being frightened by this, it filled me with a divine zeal. I decided to declare war against the enemy until the end. I wanted to snatch back every soul I could. I vowed to deliver the captives and serve the Lord with all my heart, and have been doing so ever since.

## What is the Draw into the Occult?

In my deliverance ministry I have found that no matter what type of occult an individual has been involved in, the battle against demonic influences is tremendous, and that the demonization can be quite severe. Because I was so bound, and by God's grace been set free, I want to share the wisdom I have gleaned in understanding the path to total victory.

First, it may be helpful to understand what causes a person to become susceptible to becoming ensnared by the occult. This helps us understand how best to minister to the whole person as they emerge from Satan's grasp:

1.  **Everyone involved in the occult suffers from deep rejection.**

    Rejection is the number one cause of occult involvement. A broken home, the lack of true fatherhood, all types of abuse during childhood, the early death of one or both parents, or any traumatic experience can be the cause of a deep feeling of rejection. Rejection leaves individuals longing for acceptance and significance. Satan will deceive them into believing that following his paths will provide them with both.

2.  **Those involved in the occult are generally hooked into Satan's lies through a lack of identity.**

Everyone needs to have an identity. Identity is the understanding of who we are, what our destiny is, and what is our function in this life. Of course, God created us to have our identity in Him. But, because of sin, abuse, or lack of understanding, we often do not look to God for our identity. Instead, we tend to strive to be accepted by others, to have position, to "be somebody." The cry of many souls is, "Somebody please tell me I'm worthy."

This ties back to rejection. When an individual is rejected, the need for, but lack of, true identity grows stronger. They may begin looking for identity in money and possessions or in fame or power.

The devil is looking for people just like these for whom he can promise a source of identity. A subtle voice is often sent by a messenger of Satan saying, "You are a chosen one," or "You have such unique powers, you are not like all the common people," or "You are the perfect candidate to receive all the power of the universe. You will know the future, you will have power to heal, you will master the destinies of others." What an attractive proposal to someone, rejected and with no identity!

3.  **Inner anger is a driving force.**

Here is an important truth to understand: the devil needs anger and hatred and envy as the energizers of his demonic power. That is why James states in his epistle: "But if you harbor bitter envy and selfish ambition in your hearts, do not boast about it or deny the truth. Such 'wisdom' does not come down from heaven but is earthly, unspiritual, of the devil. For where you have envy and selfish ambition, there you find disorder and every evil practice" (3:14-16, NIV).

As long as these sins remain in the heart, the devil has a major grip that allows him to torment and beat people down into deep places of anguish, depression, and despair. Those who have been tormented by demons tend to throw themselves into the pit of desolation. This is because there is so much anger and vengeance within them, they tend to punish themselves in order to relieve the inner valves of pain.

Demons love this self-destructive cycle and gladly oblige these tormented souls, drawing them even further into Satan's grip.

4.  **Satan uses imagination mixed with reality.**
    Those involved in the occult give the enemy a lot of ground in their minds. It is there that he builds his master structures; where he can use us for his evil plans. I call it the "twilight zone." This an area in the mind somewhere between the conscience and the subconscious, between the real and the unreal world, between reality and imagination.

    People who are involved in the occult have amazing experiences in their own spirits as well as in the realm of imagination. These experiences are so real that the person can no longer tell the difference between what really happened and what was just a deep trip into the imagination.

    This is so important to deal with when helping someone emerge from the occult, otherwise the devil will devastate the person with fearful and horrifying imaginations and dreams. For true deliverance to occur, the person needs to renounce the power they have given the devil to operate in and from their minds.

## Freeing Captive Souls

Whether you are one who is emerging from the occult, or one called to setting these captives free, here are some important steps along the path to freedom:

1. **A truthful encounter with the sacrifice of Christ.**
   This is the most powerful and, in fact, the only source of deliverance and salvation. We cannot avoid this encounter. Salvation and deliverance start with a conflict: The real confrontation between our sinful nature, the dark and filthy state of our soul, and the terribly painful sacrifice of Christ on our behalf. I cannot be called a Christian, a follower of Jesus, if I do not understand that each and every one of my sins bruised, chastised, and nailed Him to the cross. I crucified Christ.

   Salvation is the response, with my entire life, soul, and spirit to what Jesus did for me. When I can see my filthiness, before His purity, my shame before His perfect love, then and only then can my life be changed. The Cross has to have a weight in our hearts that will enable us to live for it and through it. This is what delivered me, and will deliver any one who encounters it.

2. **True repentance from occult involvement.**
   True repentance is not an option. It is the primary foundation of deliverance. In addition to repenting for their individual actions, there must be repentance for having been a servant of Satan and for having made Satan, instead of God,

their father. Every sin, not only practicing the occult, makes us servants of Satan. And a sinful life makes Satan our father. We all have to really gain understanding of this, if we want to succeed in our freedom. And we need to hate that condition with every cell of our body.

3. **Want deliverance with the whole heart.**

Unfortunately, and I believe because of ignorance, many people masochistically enjoy the torment of demons. It is their way of controlling others. By always being the victim, they draw the attention and the sympathy of others. This happens when people have never made God the true center and the number one focus in their lives. They are totally centered in themselves. Whatever happens to them takes on paramount importance.

What they ignore is by doing that, they will never be delivered and they will always serve Satan in his purposes of making everybody around them miserable. They have to desire deliverance with their whole heart because they love God and love the ones around them.

The devil will always try to attack the children of God. He comes to steal, to kill, and to destroy. And this is not only those who once served him through the occult, but any child of God. But God has put in each and every one of us divine anger. This is the very wrath of God to despise and destroy every work of the enemy. We need to learn to cast him out with divine anger once and for all.

4. **Confess and break all covenants made with the devil.**

Confessing sins to one another is essential for deliverance. James 5:16 says: "Confess your faults to one another, and pray one for another, that ye may be healed" (KJV).

General confessions to God in privacy don't work for deliverance from the occult. It is crucial that those involved in the occult confess their sin to another in as much detail as possible. They need to ask the Holy Spirit to help them remember every time they asked a favor from a deity in the occult or any time they paid someone to do a "work." This may take some time, but it will help leave no stone unturned.

Then, once these have been confessed, they need to (1) break the covenants; (2) cancel the works; (3) renounce and cast out every deity; (4) break soul and spiritual ties with every ceremony and the one(s) who performed it; and (5) burn every object, garment, piece of jewelry, or idol used to participate in these ceremonies.

## 5.  Renounce the deities of voodoo.

If there has been specific involvement in voodoo, they need to renounce Legbas or Elegua, Yemaya or Erzulli, Obatala, Shango, Dambalah, Ochung, Ogun, Orula, Olofi, Olla, all "Loas" (voodoo spirits), and all the spirits of the dead that work along with them.

I am a testimony. I stand as someone who has been completely freed from the occult. The Son of Man has come to destroy all the works of the enemy, and He is still able, if you allow him to do it in your life.

The anointing of the Lord God is upon Jesus to set the captives free. My prayer is that these words, joined with His mighty presence, will help you to come out from the horrible bondages of evil you may be under. It *is* possible. I am God's witness of His amazing grace and power, and I will live to the very last day of my life committed to destroy the works of the devil.

To God be the glory for the magnificent salvation He performed in my life!  He can do the same for you!

# Subject Index

sin(s),  31, 102-103
sons of Sceva,  27
sorcerer(s),  15
sorcery,  48
sparrow,  45
spell(s),  14-15, 40, 48
spiritism,  46-48, 56, 77
spiritist(s),  15
Stevens, Selwyn,  49-50, 52
succubus,  25-26
superstition,  42-45
Sytsema, Rebecca Wagner,  52

**T**
Taoism,  16
Theosophical Society,  70
third eye,  17-18
2 Timothy 3:5,  70
Transcendental Meditation,  16-
  17
Travis, Paul,  77
Trevelyan, Sir George,  71

**U**
U.S. Strategic Prayer Network,
  8, 34
Umbanda,  15
*Unmasking Freemasonry*,  49-
  50, 52

**V**
Venezuela,  24
Voice of the Light Ministries,
  90
voodoo,  15, 23, 91-105
voodoo, deities of,  104

**W**
Wagner, C. Peter,  10, 59
Wagner, Doris M.,  7, 10
warlock(s),  15, 93

white magic,  19, 48
White, Tom,  60
Wicca,  16, 71
witch(es),  15, 21-22, 23, 27
witchcraft,  11, 19, 21-33, 37,
  66, 71
witchdoctor(s),  15, 23
*Witches*,  14-15
wizard(s),  21-22

**Y**
Yemaya,  104
yoga,  16, 17-18
*Yoruba*,  61-63